RUSSIAN TSARS

Text
Boris Antonov

Translation
Kenneth MacInnes

Design
Piotr Kanaikin

Photographs
Valentin Baranovsky, Roman Benjaminson,
Leonid Bogdanov, Serguei Chistobaev,
Pavel Demidov, Vladimir Denisov,
Vladimir Dorokhov, Alexander Kashnitsky,
Leonard Kheifets, Artur Kirakozov,
Boris Manushin, Vladimir Melnikov,
Yury Molodkovets, Alexander Petrosian,
Nikolai Rakhmanov, Viktor Savik,
Georgy Shablovsky, Nikolai Shabulin,
Yvgeny Siniaver, Vladimir Terebenin,
Oleg Trubsky, Vasily Vorontsov

Editor
Irina Kharitonova, Irina Lvova

English text editor
Elena Shrubelova

Computer layout
Nina Sokolova

Colour correction
Viacheslav Bykovski, Vladimir Kniazev,
Alexander Kongiastov, Tatiana Krakovskay,
Alexander Ptuckov, Dmitry Trofimov,
Serguei Vytovel

Includes illustration from the private
collections of Igor Filimonov
and Dmitry Mathn (St Petersburg)

ISBN 978-5-93893-109-6 (Softcover edition)
ISBN 978-5-93893-308-X (Hardcover edition)

Reflecting on the history of Russia, a country straddling two continents, one comes to the conclusion that it combines features of Eastern despotism and Western civilisation — an explosive cocktail inevitably influencing the character of the Russian autocracy. We trace our tale of Russian absolutism from its original sources to its tragic finale. The first chapter is dedicated to the birth of statehood in Russia. The second is an account of the history of the Rurikid princes — the first Russian dynasty. The third tells the story of the Time of Troubles, when the state was on the verge of complete ruin. The fourth begins with the coronation of Michael Romanov and ends with the execution of the last Russian autocrat, Nicholas II, and his family. We know the names of the leaders of popular revolts, kings and khans, but we often know very little about the personalities of the Russian tsars. These men and women were exceptional in many ways. Besides ruling one of the greatest empires that the world has ever known, many were fascinating personalities in their own right. Not all of them were ideal rulers. Like all human beings, they had their own faults, passions, feelings, and habits. The only difference is that private individuals control only their own fates or those of their friends and relatives. The personal whims of a sovereign, however, can have enormous consequences for the history of the entire nation and the fate of his or her subjects and their descendants. This helps to explain our fascination with the people who, for many centuries, ruled over the Russian lands.

...... 862–1462

THE ESTABLISHMENT OF STATEHOOD. THE RURIKID PRINCES   7

...... 1462–1598

THE FIRST RUSSIAN DYNASTY. THE RURIKID PRINCES   21

...... 1598–1613
THE TIME OF TROUBLES. INTERREGNUM   43

...... 1613–1918
THE SECOND RUSSIAN DYNASTY. THE ROMANOVS   59

THE ESTABLISHMENT OF STATEHOOD. THE RURIKID PRINCES

862–1462

This period began with the unification of the Eastern Slavs under the authority of the princes of Kiev and the creation of a powerful state known as Kievan Rus. The country stretched from the Gulf of Finland in the north to the Black Sea in the south; from the Carpathian Mountains in the West to the rivers Don and Volga in the east. Between the second half of the ninth century and the early twelfth century, the state flourished. An important factor was the authority of the grand prince, who controlled the great waterway "from the Varanghians to the Greeks." In the early twelfth century, the power of the grand prince began to weaken and the country split up into a number of independent states, which broke away from Kiev. There was nothing unusual about this; Western Europe had undergone a similar process in the ninth century. Russia faced an additional problem, however, with the westward movement of the Tatar-Mongol hordes. For several centuries, Rus lived under the Tatar-Mongol yoke, halting the country's natural development. The foreign invaders were eventually overthrown and the Russian people began rebuilding their state around Moscow, which had, by the mid-fifteenth century, become the centre of the reunified nation.

The Election of a Prince (Prince Meeting Militia Elders and the People of a Slavonic Town in the Eleventh Century).
Artist: Alexei Kivshenko

First Meeting of Prince Igor and Olga.
Artist: Vasily Sazonov

First Rurikid Princes. Mural from the eastern wall of the Palace of Facets in the Moscow Kremlin.
Artists: Belousov brothers from Palekh

Rurik

Igor

Olga

The history of the formation of the Russian state begins with Prince Rurik, the member of a Slavonic tribe inhabiting the southern shores of the Baltic Sea and the island of Ruegen. For over seven centuries, his descendants ruled several Russian princedoms and then the entire country.

Various unions of the East Slavonic tribes displayed all the attributes of statehood. The best known are the tribal unions headed by Kyi (founder of the town of Kiev in the late fifth century) and Gostomysl (head of a Slavonic tribal association based around Novgorod in the ninth century). Russian statehood is generally regarded as beginning in 859, when Prince

Rurik was invited to rule Novgorod, in an attempt to stave off internecine warfare. His reign dates from 862. Two years later, Askold and Dir liberated Kiev from the Khazars.

Rurik died in 879, leaving an infant son called Igor. Before his death, he named his relative Oleg as his successor. In 882, Prince Oleg prepared to wage war

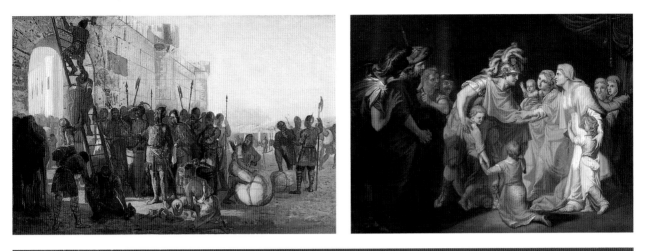

Oleg Fastening his Shield to the Gates of Constantinople.
Artist: Nikolai Bodarevsky

Grand Prince Svyatoslav Kissing his Mother and Children on Returning to Kiev from the Danube.
Artist: Ivan Akimov

against Askold and Dir in Kiev. He invited the two men to his camp, where they were murdered. Two churches were later built on the site of their graves — the Church of St Nicholas for Askold and the Church of St Irene for Dir. Oleg was crowned prince of Kiev and the city became the capital of Old Russia or Kievan Rus. Kievan Rus was surrounded by aggressive neighbours and was often invaded by the Norman tribes living to the north. The Varanghians (Vikings) penetrated deep into the heart of Russia, sailing large boats from the Gulf of Finland down the rivers Neva and Volkov, plundering and killed the inhabitants of the great waterway "from the Varanghians to the Greeks." This was a network of rivers running through the entire territory of Kievan Rus, linking northern and southern Europe. The country was attacked from the east by the Khazars, a nomadic tribe living between the rivers Volga and Don.

Svyatoslav

Alexander Pushkin describes the period of constant warfare with Khazars in his poem *The Song of Prince Igor*: "Oleg, the wise prince, again rose to arm, / And cried: 'Vengeance on the ruthless horde / Of raiding Khazars! Their field and farm / My men shall put to fire and sword!'"

The Pechenegs came from Central Asia and inhabited the lands bordering on the Black Sea. They often invaded the country on their fast horses, burning, killing and carrying off slaves. The Pechenegs once besieged Kiev, but were unable to overcome the city walls and the heroic defence of the citizens. Kievan Rus thus acted as a bulwark, saving central and western Europe from invasion by the nomadic tribes of Asia. Kievan Rus had strained relations with the Byzantine Empire. Slavs were highly valued in the Byzantine slave markets and the Byzantine emperors cast covetous eyes on the rich Russian lands. The two countries fought a series of wars. In 911, Prince Oleg signed a peace treaty giving Russian merchants the right to trade without customs or taxes in the Byzantine capital, Constantinople.

Igor's son, Prince Svyatoslav, continued to strengthen the Russian state. He defeated the Khazars and the Volga Bolgars and repulsed the attacks of the Pechenegs. In 972, however, he was killed at the Dnieper rapids, after falling into a Pecheneg trap planned by Byzantium. Svyatoslav's skull was made into a gold-plated goblet for the Pecheneg khan, who drank from it at banquets.

9

Vladimir and Rogneda. Artist: Anton Losenko
Prince Vladimir and Rogneda. Chrome lithograph
Grand Prince Vladimir Choosing a Religion. Artist: Johann Leberecht Eggink
Baptism of Prince Vladimir. Detail. Artist: Victor Vasnetsov

Vladimir

Vladimir was the son of Prince Svyatoslav Igorevich of Kiev and a woman called Malusha. In 970, he was elected the prince of Novgorod. Six years later, he learnt that one of his brothers, Yaropolk, had murdered another, Oleg, at the instigation of his Uncle Dobrynya. Vladimir assembled an army of Varanghians and marched on Kiev. On the way, he defeated the Polovtsian prince, Rogvold, and took his daughter Rogneda (Yaropolk's bride) as his wife. Vladimir then sent hired assassins to Kiev, where they murdered Yaropolk. He thus became the grand prince of Kiev at the age of thirty-three. Vladimir fought a series of wars against the enemies of Kievan Rus. He defeated the Poles and the Volga Bolgars and overcame the Radimich, Pechenegs, Khazars, Livonians and Estonians. After winning these wars, Vladimir decided to enjoy the peace. He was famed for his lavish banquets and other entertainments. The prince was passionate about women and had over eight-hundred wives from different nations. As these women practised different religions, his neighbours hoped to use them to convert Vladimir and his people to their own faith. After studying the different religions and sending emissaries to various lands, Vladimir's choice fell on the Greek Orthodox Church.

Under Svyatoslav's son, Prince Vladimir, Kievan Rus extended from the River Bug to the Baltic Sea. The prince is responsible for introducing Christianity to Russia, with important consequences for the future development of the nation. In 988, he followed the example of his grandmother, Princess Olga, who had been baptised at the age of fifty in Constantinople.

Prince Vladimir wanted to do more than just borrow the religion of the Byzantine Empire. Planning to conquer the entire country, he captured the port of Korsun (Chersonesos), the most important trading post on the Black Sea. Vladimir wrote to the Byzantine emperor, Basil II, demanding his sister Anna in marriage. In the event of refusal, he threatened to invade Constantinople. The emperor gave in to his demands and sent Anna to Korsun, accompanied by a group of courtiers and priests.

These events are described by Russian poet Alexei Tolstoy:

Baptism of Prince Vladimir. Artist: Fedor Bronnikov
Baptism of Rus. Artist: Vasily Perov
Grand Prince Vladimir. Detail. Artist: Victor Vasnetsov

The Greeks saw vessels in the sea,
The army crowding at their walls.
To anyone who listened,
Up and down there went the call:
"A great woe will befall us all —
Vladimir come to be christened!"

Vladimir and Anna were married in Korsun, where the prince was baptised as Basil. When he returned to Kiev, he threatened to kill anyone who did not convert to Christianity. The prince destroyed pagan idols and temples, building churches in their place. In 988, his family and the entire city of Kiev were baptised in a place called Kreschatik. So in the late tenth century, Kievan Rus adopted Christianity as its official religion, bringing political stability and a unique material and spiritual culture.

The prince was known as "Vladimir the Fair Sun" for his efforts in uniting and strengthening the Russian state, building new towns and introducing a new faith and culture. In the thirteenth century, he was canonised by the Russian Orthodox Church and ranked equal to the apostles. Catherine the Great later founded the Order of St Vladimir in his memory. The adoption of Christianity brought culture and learning to Kievan Rus. Religious schools were opened, churches were built and decorated with frescoes and ornaments of silver and gold. When Vladimir's son, Prince Yaroslav of Novgorod, broke away from Kiev, however, Vladimir declared him an outlaw and raised an army against him. He died on the way to Novgorod, at the village of Berestov on 15 July 1015. When two of Vladimir's sons — Boris and Gleb — were later murdered by their cousin, Prince Svyatopolk, they were canonised as the first Russian saints.

St Petersburg — the spiritual heir of Kievan Rus and capital of the Russian Empire — kept alive the memory of Prince Vladimir. In 1766, Antonio Rinaldi began building a cathedral in his honour in the Mokrushi district of the city (now Dobrolyubov Prospekt). A fire broke out in 1784, before the church was finished, and work was completed by Ivan Starov. St Vladimir's Cathedral was officially consecrated on 1 October 1789, a year after the eight-hundredth anniversary of the adoption of Christianity.

St Vladimir's Cathedral is one of the largest places of worship in St Petersburg. Capable of holding up to three thousand people, it is flanked by a three-tier bell-tower over fifty yards in height. The altar of the central side-chapel is decorated with copies of Victor Vasnetsov's *Holy Communion* murals in St Vladimir's Cathedral in Kiev. Three icons of St Vladimir stand in the altar of the Dormition Side-Chapel.

On 22 July 1845, Tsar Nicholas I made the cathedral the official place of worship of the Order of St Vladimir. The emblem of the order was placed above the main entrance. Every year, on 22 September, a special service is performed in memory of Prince Vladimir. From 1928 to 1941, the cathedral was the seat of the bishop of Leningrad. In 1940, the miracle-working icon of the Mother of God of Kazan was transferred to the church.

11

Boris and Gleb. Icon. 14th century
Yaroslav the Wise. Reading the *Russian Pravda* (Justice) to the People. Artist: Alexei Kivshenko
Anna Yaroslavna. Statue at St Vincent's Monastery, France
Boris. Detail from *Boris and Gleb* (mid-14th century)

Yaroslav the Wise

The reign of Prince Yaroslav the Wise — Vladimir's son — was the golden age of Kievan Rus. He founded the town of Yaroslavl on the River Volga and enjoyed a great victory over the Pechenegs, putting an end to their constant raids on the Russian lands. The borders of the country stretched from the Gulf of Finland in the north to the River Danube in the south and from the Carpathian Mountains in the west to the River Don in the east.

Prince Yaroslav employed the principle of marriage to integrate Kievan Rus with the rest of Europe. He married the daughter of King Olaf Skötkonung of Sweden, whose dowry was the province of Karelia. His daughters married the rulers of France (Henry I), Hungary (Andrew I) and Norway (Harold III). Yaroslav's sister, Dobronega (Maria), married King Casimir of Poland, while his son Vsevolod married the daughter of the Byzantine Emperor Constantine Monomachus. Yaroslav's granddaughter Eupraxia was the wife of the Holy Roman emperor Henry IV. Foreign powers sought alliances with Kievan Rus. Old Russian culture flourished under Yaroslav the Wise. The prince built St Sofia's Cathedral and new city walls with the Golden Gates. Kiev boasted around four hundred churches. The Russian school of religious painting and architecture also flourished. Schools were opened at monasteries. Perhaps the most important innovation was the formation of a code of laws entitled the *Russian Pravda* (Justice). Any citizen breaking the law had to pay a fine, depending on the seriousness of the crime. Although the new codex outlawed the practice of blood feuds in Russia, it was now possible to simply compensate the relatives of a murdered man, as each murder entailed a fine. Anyone killing a common man had to pay his relatives five grivnas. The death of a prince's servant or soldier carried a fine of eighty grivnas. Although the *Russian Justice* was far from perfect, any legislation was better than none at all.

Before his death in 1054, Yaroslav divided the country up between his five sons and one nephew. The resulting internecine warfare weakened the state, leading to the decline of Kiev and the emergence of several independent princedoms — Chernihiv, Pereyaslavl, Murom, Ryazan, Rostov-Suzdal, Galicia, Vladimir-Volhynia, Polotsk, Turov-Pinsk, Tmutarakan and the lands of Novgorod and Pskov. Each small state was ruled by a branch of the Rurikid family. The result was many years of incessant warfare, between first the sons and then the grandsons of Prince Yaroslav.

Ordeal by Fire. Trial during the Times of the *Russian Pravda* (Justice). Artist: Ivan Bilibin

Greek Ambassadors Bearing Gifts to Prince Vladimir Monomachus.
Artist: Alexei Kivshenko

Gleb. Detail from *Boris and Gleb* (mid-14th century)

Vladimir Monomachus

In the early twelfth century, Vladimir-Suzdal (or Rostov-Suzdal) was the most powerful state between the rivers Oka and Volga. Such new towns as Yuriev-Polskoi, Zvenigorod, Pereyaslavl-Zalessky, Kostroma, Dmitrov, Nizhny Novgorod, Moscow and Galich emerged, alongside the older cities of Rostov, Suzdal, Vladimir and Yaroslavl. Suzdal was ruled by Vladimir Monomachus's son Yury, who received the epithet of "Dolgoruky" ("long arms") for his constant incursions into neighbouring territories. Yury Dolgoruky founded Moscow in 1147. The first mention of the town in the chronicles dates from 4 April 1147, when Yury held a banquet in honour of his ally, Prince Svyatoslav of Chernihiv. At the banquet, Svyatoslav presented him with a rare and expensive gift — the skin of a snow leopard.

The town of Moscow developed out of the village of Kuchkovo, which stood at the confluence of two rivers — the Moscow and the Neglinnaya. The village was owned by a boyar or nobleman called Stepan Kuchka. Yury Dolgoruky killed the owner, married his daughter to his son Andrei and took over the village, which he renamed Moscow. A town was built here in 1156. In 1157, Yury died and was succeeded by his son Andrei, who moved the capital to Vladimir on Klyazma. He was known as Prince Andrei of Bogolyubovo, after his new white-stoned palace in Bogolyubovo. Kiev lost its former role as the capital of the entire nation and the centre of Russian political life moved to the north-east. Calling himself the "grand prince of all Rus," Andrei attempted to hold sway over all the other princedoms, but was ultimately murdered in Bogolyubovo in 1174.

One of the most important rivals of Vladimir-Suzdal was Novgorod the Great near Lake Ilmen. Stretching as far as the White Lake and the rivers Onega, North Dvina and Ural, Novgorod stood on the trade route "from the Varanghians to the Greeks." This state was ruled by a popular assembly known as the *veche*, which had the power to declare war, sign peace and elect its own burgomaster or *posadnik*. The *veche* elected such other officials as the head of the army and the archbishop, who was also responsible for foreign policy and finances. The army was commanded by a prince, who was not allowed to own land in Novgorod or to interfere in politics. He was not even allowed to live in Novgorod, but had his own residence called Gorodische outside the city.

Novgorod was a leading centre of the arts and crafts. The local bone and wood carvers, jewellers and blacksmiths were famed throughout and beyond Russia. The streets of Novgorod were paved and had wooden sewage pipes. Surviving birch-bark

13

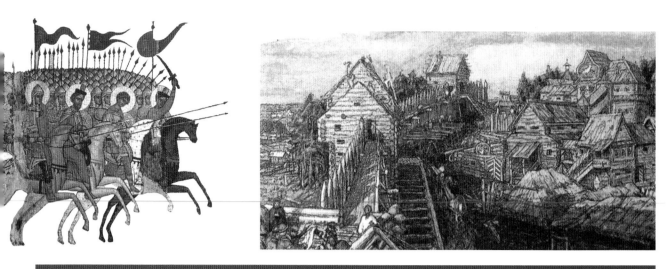

Novgorodian Host. Detail from *Battle between the Novgorodians and Suzdalites*
(Miracle of the Icon of the Mother of God of the Holy Sign)
Building the First Walls of the Kremlin in the Twelfth Century.
Artist: Apollinary Vasnetsov

Yury Dolgoruky

Andrei of Bogolyubovo

documents demonstrate the high level of literacy in Novgorod. The town had many famous churches, including St Sofia's Cathedral (built in the eleventh century) and the Church of the Saviour on Nereditsa (destroyed during the Second World War and now restored).

Galicia-Volhynia in the south-west of the country was another important state, resulting from the union of Galicia and Volhynia under Prince Roman Mstislavich in 1199. Stretching as far as the Carpathian Mountains, Galicia-Volhynia occupied the territory between the rivers Dniester and Pruth and included such large towns as Galich, Vladimir-Volhynia, Kholm, Berestye (Brest), Lviv and Przemysl. These lands were so large that Pope Innocent III allowed Prince Roman to take the title of king. Galicia-Volhynia was a major centre of Old Russian architecture, painting and crafts, famed for its illustrated manuscript books in handsome leather bindings decorated with gold and precious stones. The prince built a magnificent palace and chapel in the town of Galich.

The development of Russian culture and statehood was suddenly interrupted in the thirteenth century, when the country was invaded by the Tatars and Mongols.

In 1223, a Russian army was defeated on the River Kalka near the Sea of Azov. After the battle, the Tatars held a victory banquet on wooden boards placed on top of wounded prisoners. Twenty years later, Khan Baty invaded Russia and established the Tatar-Mongol yoke. For more than two centuries, Russian towns and villages were burnt and pillaged, while the people were murdered, raped and enslaved.

The state founded by Khan Baty was known as the Golden Horde. The capital of the Golden Horde was the town of Sarai on the River Volga, not far from the modern-day city of Volgograd. The capital was later transferred further up the River Volga, to a place known as New Sarai. The Golden Horde controlled much of Central Asia, Kazakhstan, the Crimea, the rivers Volga and Dnieper and north-east Rus. Although the Tatar-Mongol hordes did not reach Novgorod, the city was still obliged to pay tribute.

Rus suffered under the Tatar-Mongol yoke. The population was forced to give up one-tenth of its property and pay tribute in the form of bread, cattle and money. The tribute was collected by special tax collectors called *baskaki*. Anyone refusing to pay was immediately sold into slavery. The Russian princes were forced to bow down before their overlord, the Tatar khan, and give him expensive presents. The khan permitted them to keep the title of prince and later let them collect the tribute themselves.

The Golden Horde began to weaken in the fourteenth century. In the second half of the century, there were twenty-five khans in the space of twenty-three years. Many were murdered by rivals. In the 1370s, the Golden Horde was headed by a military commander called Mamai, until his defeat at the Battle of Kulikovo.

Suzdalite Host. Detail from *Battle between the Novgorodians and Suzdalites*
(Miracle of the Icon of the Mother of God of the Holy Sign)

After the Battle between Igor Svyatoslavovich and the Polovtsians.
Artist: Victor Vasnetsov

Campaign of Prince Igor Svyatoslavovich

Mamai fled to the Crimea, but was caught and killed. As the Tatar-Mongol yoke weakened, Moscow grew in strength. Although the raids on the Russian lands continued, the days of the Golden Horde were numbered. Russia's neighbours took advantage of the Mongol invasion to invade the country from the north. The western territories were invaded by Poland and Lithuania. The Lithuanians annexed the Dnieper region, Chernigov and Minsk. Galicia was swallowed up by Poland. Novgorod led the resistance and Prince Alexander Nevsky defeated the Swedes in 1240 and the Teutonic Knights in 1242. (Alexander Nevsky was canonised by the Russian Orthodox Church in 1547.)

In 1240, German and Danish knights crossed the border and occupied a large portion of north-west Rus, including the town of Pskov. Led by Alexander Nevsky, the Russians recaptured several towns and marched on Lake Chudskoye (Peipus), blocking the enemy's advance towards Novgorod. The Battle of Lake Chudskoye — also known as the Battle on the Ice — was fought on 5 April 1242.

Alexander Nevsky Accepting Papal Legates. Artist: Henryk Siemiradzki
Battle of the Neva. Alexander Nevsky Injuring the Face of Birger
Teutonic Knight and Knight of the Sword-Bearers (Allies of the Teutonic Order)
Battle on the Ice (Battle of Lake Chudskoye)

The Russian forces surrounded and crushed the German knights. The Battle on the Ice was the first major victory of infantry over cavalry. The Russians managed to surround' and rout a much superior force, capturing fifty knights and killing more than five hundred.

Victory at the Battle of Chudskoye put an end to the eastern raids of the knights of the Teutonic Order, which had gone on for several centuries with the tacit but substantial support of the Papal Curia.

The Russian resistance to the Mongol invasion weakened the power of the enemy forces, saving Europe from suffering the same fate. Gradually, the years of enslavement were overcome and Russian statehood began to revive. Ruled from 1325 by Prince Ivan Kalita ("Money Bag"),

St Alexander Nevsky in the Horde. Artist: Henryk Siemiradzki
Battle of Eupaty Kolovrat
Moscow Kremlin under Ivan Kalita. Artist: Apollinary Vasnetsov
Alexander Nevsky. Centre of the *St Alexander Nevsky* triptych.
Artist: Pavel Korin

Daniil of Moscow   **Ivan Kalita**

Moscow emerged as the new centre. It was the official residence of the head of the church (metropolitan) and the centre of the Russian Orthodox religion. The town grew throughout the fourteenth century.

In 1378, Moscow refused to pay its annual tribute to the Golden Horde. Khan Mamai decided to punish the country by invading with a large Tatar-Mongol army, which was defeated by Ivan Kalita's grandson, Prince Dmitry of Moscow. In 1380, Khan Mamai invaded with a new and stronger force. Prince Dmitry led the Russian resistance and defeated the Mongols at the Battle of Kulikovo near the source of the River Don.

The Battle of Kulikovo — also known as the Slaughter of Mamai — was fought on 8 September 1380. The battle was named after the meadowland lying between the rivers Don, Nepryadva and Krasivaya Mecha in the south-west of modern-day Tula Region. The Russian forces were commanded by Grand Prince Dmitry Ivanovich of Moscow and Vladimir. The Tatar-Mongol hordes were led by Mamai. The forces were more or less equal, with 100,000 to 150,000 men on each side.

The battle was a bitter struggle between robbers and pillagers on the one side and an army fighting for the freedom and life of the nation on the other. The two sides clashed on the day of the Nativity of the Blessed Virgin.

Grand Prince Dmitry Visiting St Sergius of Radonezh before Advancing on the Tatars. Artist: Alexei Kivshenko
Single Combat of Alexander Peresvet and Temir-Murza (Chelubey)
For the Native Land. Artist: Nikolai Prisekin
Grand Prince Dmitry Donskoi of Moscow. Detail. Unknown Artist

Before the battle began, the Russian army prayed before the holy icon of the Mother of God of the Don, vowing to fight to the end. Although Prince Dmitry managed to defeat and scatter Mamai's army, the Russians also suffered heavy losses. When Mamai's successor, Tokhtamysh, attacked Moscow in 1382, there was no one left to defend the city. Tokhtamysh sacked the town and forced Rus to pay a large tribute.

On the feast-day of St Demetrius of Solun, patron saint of soldiers, St Sergius of Radonezh performed a special mass in memory of those killed at the Battle of Kulikovo. Every year, on 8 November, the Russian Orthodox Church holds a special service called St Demetrius Commemoration Day in honour of those who died fighting the Golden Horde at the Battle of Kulikovo. St Sergius of Radonezh contributed to the Russian victory at the Battle of Kulikovo, supporting Prince Dmitry with his advice and prayers. He called on all the Russian princes to submit to the command of the grand prince of Moscow. Before setting off for Kulikovo, Prince Dmitry visited Sergius to receive his blessing. The saint prophesied his victory and survival. Approaching the River Don, Dmitry hesitated, unsure whether or not to cross the river. He took the decision to cross upon receipt of a letter from St Sergius, urging him to attack the Tatars

Morning at Kulikovo Field. Artist: Alexander Bubnov
Militiaman and the Khan of the Golden Horde

as quickly as possible. In 1389, the prince asked the saint to countersign his spiritual testament, establishing a new order of succession, whereby the throne passed to the sovereign's eldest son.

St Sergius of Radonezh was canonised by the Russian Orthodox Church in 1452. Prince Dmitry became known as "Dmitry Donskoi" ("of the Don") in honour of his victory at the Battle of Kulikovo. During his reign, Moscow emerged as the leading Russian princedom. When Dmitry died, he passed the throne to Basil I — for the first time without the sanction of the Golden Horde.

Although the foreign yoke still continued and the Mongols captured a series of towns and villages, including Moscow, victory at the Battle of Kulikovo was of tremendous psychological importance. The Russians no longer feared the Mongol hordes. For his services to his religion and his role in the victory, Prince Dmitry Donskoi was canonised by the Russian Orthodox Church.

Simeon the Proud

Andrei Rublev was a famous Russian icon-painter who lived around the same time as Dmitry Donskoi. He decorated many Russian churches, including the Annunciation Cathedral in the Moscow Kremlin, the Dormition Cathedral at Vladimir, the Trinity Cathedral in Sergiev Posad and the Cathedral of the Saviour at the Andronik Monastery. Rublev was famous for his sublime and inspired images in such works as *Old Testament Trinity*.

The majority of Russian lands were united under Grand Prince Ivan III of Moscow. The Tatar-Mongol yoke was finally overthrown at the Battle of the River Ugra in 1480. Ivan III regarded himself as the successor to the Byzantine emperors and adopted their coat of arms — a black double-headed eagle on a golden background. National laws were introduced throughout the entire country. In 1497, a new codex introduced the institution of serfdom in Russia. Moscow was rebuilt as the capital of the new, centralised state. The Kremlin was surrounded by high stone walls and turrets, while a new palace was built from stone. The Italian architect Aristotle Fioravanti designed the Dormition Cathedral, while the Palace of Facets was built to host banquets and receptions for foreign kings and ambassadors.

Basil I

The country was finally united under Grand Prince Basil III, who annexed Pskov and Ryazan and took Smolensk back from Lithuania. Although inhabited by many different nationalities, the new state became known as Russia.

In January 1547, at the age of seventeen, Ivan IV crowned himself in the Dormition Cathedral. In doing so, the new ruler made an important announcement. He declared that he would no longer be called grand prince, but the "tsar of all the Russias".

Basil II

THE FIRST RUSSIAN DYNASTY. THE RURIKID PRINCES

1462–1598

The family of Prince Rurik subdivided into a large number of branches, beginning with the prince's great-grandson, Grand Prince Vladimir of Kiev. Vladimir's son, Yaroslav the Wise, divided the country between his different sons. The most important branch was the offspring of his second son, Prince Svyatoslav. In the late twelfth century, his great-grandson, Grand Prince Vsyevolod Yuryevich "Great Nest" of Vladimir, was the dominant Russian prince. His descendants became the grand princes and tsars of Moscow. The Rurikid dynasty came to an end when Tsar Fedor I died in 1598. The descendants of Prince Rurik ruled Rus for seven centuries. Many aristocratic families traced their ancestry from the prince. They took their surnames — Odoyevsky, Mosalsky, Gorchakov, Baryatinsky, Obolensky, Repnin, Volkonsky, Kropotkin, Shakhovskoi and Dolgorukov — from the names of their hereditary estates or the nicknames of their ancestors. Besides ruling the country, Rurik's offsprings also occupied important political, legal and military posts. More than ten thousand of his descendants are now scattered throughout Russia and the world.

Grand Prince
Ivan III Vasilyevich
of Moscow and All Rus
1440–1505

Parents:

Grand Prince **Basil II Vasilyevich the Dark** and Grand Princess **Maria Yaroslavna** (granddaughter of Prince Vladimir Andreyevich the Brave).

Wives:

Maria Borisovna Tverskaya. They were married when Ivan was twelve and Maria was ten. Died on 22 April 1467. According to rumours, she was poisoned.

Zoe (Sophie Fominichna) Paleologus. Niece of the last Byzantine emperor. Married Ivan on 12 November 1472 and died on 7 April 1503.

Children of Ivan III and Maria Tverskaya:

Ivan the Younger was born on 15 February 1458. From 1471, several documents call him "grand prince", alongside his father. He died in suspicious circumstances at the age of thirty-two (7 March 1490). Married Elena, daughter of Stefan III the Great, hospodar of Moldova (6 January 1483). Ivan the Younger and Elena had a son, Dmitry (10 October 1483), who was crowned grand prince in the cap and shoulder mantle of Monomachus at the Dormition Cathedral (4 February 1498). The second wife of Ivan III, Zoe Paleologus, intrigued against Dmitry. Ivan III forbade Dmitry's name to be remembered in the liturgical prayers (11 April 1502) and crowned his second son as Grand Prince Basil III of Moscow (14 April 1502).

Children of Ivan III and Zoe Paleologus:

The first two children died in infancy.

Basil (see Basil III).

Yury was born on 23 March 1480 and died in 1536.

Dmitry was born on 6 October 1481 and died in 1521.

Simeon was born on 21 March 1487 and died in 1518.

Andrei was born on 5 August 1490 and died in 1537.

Elena was born on 8 April 1484 and died in 1513. Married the future King Alexander the Jagiellonian of Poland (15 February 1495).

Feodosia was born on 29 May 1485 and died in 1501. Married Prince Vasily Danilovich Kholmsky (1500).

Eudokia was born in 1492 and died in 1513. Married a Tatar prince who converted to Christianity and took the name of Peter (25 January 1506).

...... 1480s

In the fifteenth century, the Golden Horde weakened and split up into different parts. Several sections broke away to form the independent khanates of Kazan, Astrachan, Crimea, Siberia and the Grand Horde. Under Ivan III, Rus stopped paying tribute to the Tatar-Mongols. Khan Akhmat of the Grand Horde attempt to reconquer Rus, but was defeated.

Ivan III was tall and slim. Because of a slight stoop, he was known as "Ivan Gorbaty" or "Hunchback". Although handsome, he had a stern gaze, often causing women to faint when he stared at them. Ivan was cautious, slow and calculating in affairs of state. Anything begun was taken to its logical conclusion. Daring and courage were not encouraged. Pity was not part of his character.

During the reign of Grand Prince Ivan III, Moscow increased five times in size. When he ascended the throne, he ruled over 400,000 square kilometres; by the time he died, his domains exceeded two million square kilometres. Ivan annexed Yaroslavl in 1468, Perm in 1472, Rostov in 1474, Novgorod in 1478, Tver in 1485 and Vyatka in 1489. Many west Russian lands broke away from Lithuania in 1503 to become part of Muscovite Rus. The annexations of Novgorod, Vyatka and Perm — home to non-Russian peoples — created a multi-national state. Before he died, Ivan III divided his territory between his five sons, awarding Basil III seniority and sixty-six towns. The four younger sons were given a smaller number of towns and forbidden to strike their own coins

1471	First war between Moscow and Novgorod. Under the terms of the peace treaty, Novgorod breaks away from Lithuania and recognises the authority of Moscow.
1478	Second war between Moscow and Novgorod. Ivan III annexes Novgorod and removes the *veche* bell to Moscow.
1480	Stand-off with Khan Akhmat at the River Ugra, finally overthrowing the Tatar-Mongol yoke.
1485	Annexation of Tver.
1489	Annexation of Vyatka.
1492	Construction of a fortress at the town of Narva called Ivangorod ("Ivan's Town") to halt the aggression of the Livonian Germans.
1494	Lithuania recognises Moscow's right to Novgorod.
1497	Peasants are allowed to leave their owners in the fortnight before and after St George's (Yuriev) Day on 26 November. First codex of laws.

Ivan III Tearing Up a Document from the Khan.
Artist: Nikolai Shustov

Moscow rose from the main town of the Muscovite princedom to become the capital of the whole of Russia. Ivan built stone walls and mighty towers around the Kremlin. He invited Italian architect Aristotle Fioravanti to build a five-cupola church inside the Kremlin — the Dormition Cathedral. The Palace of Facets and a large stone palace were also constructed.

Moscow Kremlin under Ivan III.
Artist: Apollinary Vasnetsov

Martha the Mayoress. Destruction of Novgorodian Liberty under Ivan III (1478). Artist: Claudius Lebedev

or enter into diplomatic relations with other nations. Russian historian Nikolai Karamzin wrote about Ivan III: "He left a remarkably large state, with a strong people and a strong power base." In 1476, Ivan III refused to pay tribute to Khan Akhmat of the Grand Horde. Akhmat gathered an enormous army and marched on Rus. The two sides met at the River Ugra, the source of the River Oka, in 1480. Both armies stood on opposite sides of the river, neither side daring to make the first move, remaining there throughout the autumn. Suffering from cold and hunger, the Tatars decided to retreat on 11 November. This event became known as the "great stand-off on the River Ugra." In 1481, Prince Ivak of the Nogai Horde killed Khan Akhmat of the Grand Horde and the hold of the Tatar-Mongol forces crumbled.

Great Stand-Off on the River Ugra in November 1480
(Rus was finally free)

• • • • • • **1497**

In 1497, Ivan III established the official symbol of Russia — a double-headed eagle — which remained the national emblem until October 1917, when the Bolsheviks seized power. On 8 December 2000, the State Duma returned the two-headed eagle to the Russian coat of arms.

Russian
Eagle

Cupolas of the Moscow Kremlin
cathedrals

Under Ivan III, the prince of Moscow became known as the "grand prince of all Rus." In his dealings with Lithuania and the German kingdoms, the prince was the "tsar of all Rus." When addressing their ruler, the boyars called him "Ivan Vasilyevich, Sovereign and Grand Prince of All Rus." Ivan III introduced the coronation ceremony, first performed on his grandson Dmitry, when the metropolitan called Ivan the "tsar" and "autocrat."

Grand Prince Basil III Ivanovich of Moscow and All Rus
1479–1533

Parents: Grand Prince **Ivan III** and **Zoe Paleologus.**

Wives:
Solomonia Yurievna Saburova (1504). Divorced and imprisoned in a nunnery under the name of Sophie (1525).
Elena Vasilyevna Glinskaya (1526).

Children of Basil III and Elena Glinskaya:
Ivan (see Ivan the Terrible).
Yury (Georgy) was a feeble degenerate.

Moscow coat of arms

Basil III was known for his hard and tough character. He continued the policies of his father, displaying firmness, consistency and patience in his domestic and foreign policy. Basil is sometimes known as the "final gatherer of the Russian lands," as he abolished the old system of appendage principledoms, uniting the whole of Russia under his single autocratic authority. During the reign of Basil III, the Crimean Tatars launched a series of raids on Russian territory. The grand prince

In 1532, the Church of the Ascension was built in the royal village of Kolomenskoe, on the banks of the River Moscow. The church was built to celebrate the birth of the heir to the throne — the future Ivan the Terrible. More than fifty yards in height and total area, the church was the latest word in architecture, designed to symbolise Russian statehood.

tried various ways to protect his lands. One way was paying gifts known as *pominki* to the khan and princes. Basil incited the Crimeans to attack the Lithuanians, who responded by urging them to attack Russia.

In 1521, the Tatars advanced as far as Moscow. Basil was not in the capital at the time and the boyars were forced to pay a ransom demand. The Crimeans were only defeated when Khabar Simsky raised an army and routed them near Pereyaslavl-Ryazansky. Basil's behaviour was criticised by the boyars.

Basil III was suspicious of the boyars and cautious in his dealings with them. None were sentenced to death or fell into disfavour (the only exception was the relatively undistinguished Bersen Beklemishev). The prince did not like dissent and paid little attention to the duma of boyars, preferring to rely on his deacons and a small circle of trusted friends, including Ivan Shigona. He was nevertheless forced to appoint boyars to the key posts in the army and government.

1508	Signing and renewal (1513, 1524) of peace with Sweden.
1510	Annexation of Pskov.
1514	Smolensk returns to Russia after 110 years of Lithuanian rule.
1521	Annexation of Ryazan.
1523	Construction of the town of Basilsursk on the River Sura.
1524	Foundation of the Novodevichy Convent in Moscow.
1533–38	Elena Glinskaya's reign when her son was too young.
1538–47	Elena suddenly dies, inspiring rumours that she has been poisoned. Ivan is orphaned and Russia enters a period of "boyar rule".

Basil III Leading his Bride Elena Glinskaya into the Palace. Artist: Claudius Lebedev. Detail

Church of the Ascension in Kolomenskoe. 1532. Erected in honour of the birth of Ivan the Terrible

Basil III died in great pain of an abscess on 3 December 1533. Before his death, he took the habit under the name of Barlaam, giving his blessing and crown to his three-year-old son, the future Ivan the Terrible.

Grand Prince
Tsar Ivan IV Vasilyevich
the Terrible
of Moscow and All Rus
1530–1584

Parents:

Grand Prince **Basil III** and **Elena Glinskaya.**

Wives:

Anastasia, daughter of courtier Roman Yuryevich Zakharin-Koshkin. Died on 7 August 1560.

Maria Temryukovna, daughter of a Khabar prince. Married on 21 September 1561 and died on 1 September 1569.

Martha Sobakina, daughter of a merchant from Novgorod. Married on 28 October 1571 and died on 13 November 1571.

Anna Alexeyevna Koltovskaya. Married in early 1572. Two years later, banished to a nunnery and forced to take the veil under the name of Daria. Died at the Tikhvin Convent in 1626.

Maria Dolgorukova. Married in 1573, she was pushed through a hole in a frozen river for "falling in love with a man before her marriage and not telling the tsar."

Anna Petrovna Vasilchikova. Married in 1575, died in 1579 of a "chest complaint" and buried at the Suzdal Convent.

Vasilisa Melentieva. Very little is known about her, except that she is rumoured to have been buried alive along with her lover, Ivan Kolychev.

Maria Fedorovna Nagaya. Married in September 1580. Forced to take the veil under the name of Martha. Died in 1608.

Not long before he died, Ivan divorced Maria Nagaya in order to marry Lady Mary Hastings, a lady-in-waiting to Queen Elizabeth of England.

Children:

Besides those who died in infancy, Ivan had three children. He had two sons (Ivan and Fedor) by his first wife, Anastasia, and one son (Dmitry) by his last wife, Maria Nagaya.

Ivan was born in 1554. In 1581, Ivan IV killed him in a rage. His remorseful father made a large endowment to the Russian church in his memory and even planned on abdicating and retiring to a monastery.

Fedor (see Fedor I).

Dmitry was born soon after Ivan's murder in 1582. He died in suspicious circumstances in Uglich in 1591.

The cap of Monomachus was part of the regalia of the grand princes and tsars of Russia. This was a golden crown trimmed with sable and decorated with precious stones and a cross. One legend claims that it was sent to Grand Prince Vladimir I in 988 by Byzantine emperors Basil II and Constantine IX, on the occasion of his baptism and marriage to their sister Anna.

Kazan Cap of Ivan
the Terrible. 1553. Moscow

Better known as Ivan the Terrible, Ivan IV was the son of Grand Prince Basil III and Elena Glinskaya. He was born on 25 August 1530 in the village of Kolomenskoe near Moscow. When he was three, his father died and was succeeded by his mother. Elena Glinskaya was an energetic and ambitious woman who concentrated power in her own hands. Her reign was a long line of palace intrigues, power struggles and violence — all witnessed by the young prince. Elena suddenly died at the age of thirty-five in 1538, inspiring rumours that she had been poisoned. Ivan was orphaned and Russia entered a period of "boyar rule", with different clans fighting for power and murdering their rivals. Surrounded by intrigues and bloody reprisals, the young boy grew suspicious, sadistic and revengeful. At the age of thirteen, he set a pack of dogs on Prince Andrei Shuisky and enjoyed torturing people. In his later letters to Prince Kurbsky, the tsar recalls his childhood as a time of insults and humiliations. Ivan spent much of his childhood in the libraries of the tsar and metropolitan, reading books on autocratic power. On 16 January 1547, he received the chance to put this knowledge into practice when he was crowned at the Dormition Cathedral in the Moscow Kremlin. During the ceremony, Metropolitan Macarius handed him the attributes of supreme power — the cross, regalia collar and cap of Monomachus. After taking the holy sacrament, Ivan was anointed with myrrh. In 1561, he was

Tsarevich Ivan on Promenade.
Artist: Mikhail Avilov

1548	Ivan convenes the first Land Council and announces that he will henceforth be the sole judge and defender of the nation, blaming the boyars for all previous problems.
1550	Compilation of a new code of laws. Formation of the Streltsy guards.
1551	The Hundred Chapters Council approves a religious code called the *Hundred Chapters*.
1552	Conquest of Kazan.
1553	Establishment of trading relations with Britain.
1555–56	Abolition of the system of keeping officials at the expense of the local population and introduction of the Code of Service.
1556	Conquest of Astrachan.
1558–83	Livonian War to gain access to the Baltic Sea. The war ends in Russia's defeat and the loss of several territories.
1560	Resignation of the *starets* Sylvester and Alexei Adashev.
1561	Defeat of the Livonian order and the absorption of Livonia by the Polish-Lithuanian Commonwealth, the annexation of Estonia by Sweden and the island of Osel by Denmark, and the formation of the duchy of Courland.
1564	Publication of the first printed book in Russia — *Apostle*.
1565	Formation of the *oprichnina*.
1570	Conquest of Novgorod.
1571	Crimean khan Devlet-Girei sets fire to Moscow.
1574	Publication of the first Slavonic alphabet.
1578	Sudden end to executions; memorial lists of executed people are compiled and endowments are made to monasteries in memory of their souls.
1581	Start of the annexation of Siberia.
	Peasants are prohibited from traditionally leaving their owners on St George's (Yuriev) Day.
1582	Treaty of Jam Zapolski with the Polish-Lithuanian Commonwealth, depriving Russia of all claims to Livonia. Annexation of Siberia.
1583	Treaty of Plussa with Sweden, depriving Russia of Narva and other towns south of the Gulf of Finland. Death of Ivan Fedorov, first printer of Moscow.

The assimilation of the fertile lands to the south of Tula, known as the Wild Fields, began in the sixteenth century. Defensive lines were built in the region of Tula and Belgorod, consisting of heaps of timber and wooden stockades. These "timber pales" defended Russia's southern borders from the Crimean Tatars.

The Palace of Facets is the oldest secular building in Moscow. Constructed by order of Ivan III it owes its name to the decorative stonework on its east facade. It was part of the palace complex of grand princes and was used for ceremonial receptions. Most important events in Russia's history were marked here with festivities. Thus, it was here that Ivan the Terrible celebrated his victory over the city of Kazan. The interior is a spacious, almost square in form, hall with a tetrahedral pillar in the centre supporting its cross-shaped vaults.

Palace of Facets of the Moscow Kremlin.
Interior

officially recognised as "tsar" by the patriarch of Constantinople and Moscow became the successor to the Byzantine capital or the "Third Rome".

Two weeks after his coronation, Ivan married Anastasia, the daughter of Roman Zakharin-Yuriev. Now officially confirmed as the sovereign, he began to rule the country. Ivan IV had all the qualities needed to be a good tsar. He had a shrewd mind and an excellent grasp of politics and diplomacy. His hot temper and despotic nature, however, earned him the epithet of "terrible". Ivan initially relied on the help of a "select assembly", consisting of Alexei Adashev, Prince Andrei Kurbsky, Metropolitan Macarius and Father Sylvester. He also convened the Land Council (*Zemsky Sobor*), which included representatives of all classes. The tsar sought to centralise the government and to limit the power of the duma of boyars. In the early 1560s, Ivan dissolved the select assembly and persecuted the former members.

Ivan the Terrible overhauled the Russian army. The main component of the armed forces was an irregular army composed of members of the nobility. Ivan stationed a body known as the Chosen Thousand outside Moscow. This was a group of 1,070 provincial noblemen, whom the tsar hoped to rely upon. The Streltsy regiments were formed in 1550 from free citizens, who were supposed to serve all their lives. The military occupation became an hereditary profession. By 1584, around twelve thousand men served in the Streltsy regiments.

Burial Vessels from the Graves of Ivan the Terrible and Sons. 16th century

In 1552, Ivan the Terrible besieged Kazan with an army of 150,000 men, 150 large cannons and qualified engineers. Russian sappers dug under the city walls and exploded barrels of gunpowder in the tunnels. The troops then poured through the holes in the walls and captured the city after a fierce battle.

Permanent exhibition of the Moscow Armoury.
Right: Throne of Ivan the Terrible (16th century)

Seven and a half thousand were stationed in Moscow. Ivan also created a permanent artillery force. The Streltsy guards did not constitute the entire army. The main military power remained a body of public servants known as the *rat'* or "host". Each town or district was supposed to supply a certain number of volunteers from the general population. Foreigners were also invited to join the Russian army, though their numbers were not large. Cossacks patrolled and protected the Russian borders.

The separate khanates of Kazan and Astrachan emerged from the remnants of the Golden Horde. They controlled the trade along the River Volga and often invaded Russian territory. In 1552, Ivan the Terrible besieged Kazan with an army of 150,000 men, 150 large cannons and qualified engineers. Russian sappers dug under the city walls and exploded barrels of gunpowder in the tunnels. The troops then poured through the holes in the walls and captured the city after a fierce battle. In honour of the defeat of Kazan, Ivan built the Cathedral of the Intercession of the Holy Virgin on Red Square in Moscow. Popularly known as St Basil's Cathedral, the building consisted

Ivan IV Entering Kazan.
Artist: Pyotr Shamshin

Ivan IV the Terrible.
Artist: Leonid Sergeyev

In 1565, Ivan introduced a form of dictatorship known as the *oprichnina* — a state within a state under his own personal control. This personal fiefdom was ruled by the *oprichniki* — an elite corps of lifeguards who wore black robes similar to monks' habits. They tied dogs' heads and brooms to their saddles, symbolising their intention of brushing or tearing away their enemies.

Ivan the Terrible Taking a Livonian Fortress.
Artist: Pavel Sokolov-Skalya

Ivan IV Besieging a Livonian Town.
Artist: Fedor Modrov

Ivan the Terrible and Malyuta Skuratov.
Artist: Grigory Sedov

The *oprichniki* tied dogs' heads and brooms to their saddles

of nine high chapels crowned with cupolas and joined to one another by arched passageways. Construction of the church was headed by a master called Postnik Jakovlev.

Ivan's army captured Astrachan in 1556. The following year, Chuvashia and a large part of Bashkiria were absorbed by Russia. Ivan's authority was also recognised by the Nogai Horde — a nation of nomadic warriors who left the Golden Horde in the late fourteenth century. In this way, Russia took the place of the Tatar-Mongols in the Volga lands, inheriting control of the trade route along the River Vol-

Ivan the Terrible accused the boyars of poisoning his wife Anastasia and vowed to avenge her death. On 3 December 1564, he suddenly abandoned Moscow. The boyars were confused and the people were frightened. The metropolitan was sent to beg the tsar to return to the capital. Ivan agreed, but warned that he planned to chop off the heads of all his enemies. This signalled the start of his reign of terror.

Execution during the Reign of Ivan the Terrible.
Artist: Vladimir Vladimirov

Nikolai Cherkasov as Ivan the Terrible
in Sergei Eisenstein's Film *Ivan the Terrible*

ga and opening up the road to Siberia. The lands beyond the Ural Mountains, along the rivers Tobol and Irtysh, were the home of the Siberian khanate. Ivan the Terrible awarded the Stroganov family of merchants and industrialists the rights to the territories around the River Tobol. In 1581, the Stroganovs raised a Cossack army headed by Yermak Timofeyevich and invaded the Siberian khanate. Yermak defeated the forces of Khan Kuchum and occupied his capital of Kashlyk. The following year, Yermak was ambushed and killed, but the conquest of western Siberia continued. After seventeen years of fighting, Kuchum was finally defeated in 1598 and western Siberia became part of the Russian state.

Ivan's reign of terror was a period of executions, plots and open gangsterism. In 1565, he introduced a form of dictatorship known as the *oprichnina* — a state within a state under his own personal control. This personal fiefdom was ruled by the *oprichniki* — an elite corps of lifeguards who wore black robes similar to monks' habits. They tied dogs' heads and brooms to their saddles, symbolising their intention of brushing or tearing away their enemies. In 1570, the *oprichniki* murdered almost the entire population of Novgorod, including all the infants. The total number of victims was more than fifteen thousand people. Led by a man called Grigory (Malyuta) Skuratov-Belsky, the only strength of the *oprichniki* was their ability to terrorise the local population. They were unable to repel foreign invasions and in 1571 the suburbs of Moscow were burnt by the Crimean khan, Devlet-Girei. The *oprichnina* was eventually dissolved in 1572.

Believing that he was dying, Ivan the Terrible asked to be carried to his treasure room to say farewell to his magnificent jewels. Picking up several turquoises, the tsar turned to the English ambassador, Jeremy Harsey, and said: "Look how they change colour ... This means that I have been poisoned. This is a portent of death."

Ivan the Terrible Showing Treasures to the English Ambassador Harsey.
Artist: Alexander Litovchenko

Ivan the Terrible had at least eight wives. When his first wife Anastasia died in 1560, it was rumoured that she had been poisoned. In 1561, the tsar married Maria Temryuko-va, daughter of a Khabar prince. When she died in 1569, she was also rumoured to have been poisoned. In 1571, Ivan married the daughter of a merchant from Novgorod, Martha Sobakina, who died a month later. When Ivan wanted to marry for the fourth time, the Russian Orthodox Church reminded him that a man was not allowed to have more than three wives. The tsar simply disregarded the church laws, forcing the church council to grant him permission or entering into common-law marriages. In 1572, Anna Koltovskaya became the tsar's fourth wife. After living together for less than a year, she was banished to a nunnery, where she spent the next fifty-four years of her life. In 1573, Ivan married Maria Dolgorukova, who was pushed through a hole in a frozen river for "falling in love with a man before her marriage and not telling the tsar." Ivan's next wife was Princess Anna Vasilchikova. They married in 1575

Ivan the Terrible's Vision of the Ghosts of his Murder Victims.
Artist: Baron Mikhail von Klodt

Ivan the Terrible once entered the apartments of his son Ivan and encountered his daughter-in-law, whom he considered to be immodestly dressed. He began to beat the pregnant woman, causing a miscarriage. When his son came running to the woman's cries, the tsar struck him on the head with his staff, killing his son.

Ivan the Terrible and his Son Ivan on 16 November 1581.
Artist: Ilya Repin

and lived together for four years, until Anna died of a "chest complaint" in 1579. Ivan's seventh wife was Vasilisa Melentieva. Very little is known about her, except that she is rumoured to have been buried alive along with her lover, Ivan Kolychev. In autumn 1580, the tsar married his eighth wife, a boyar's daughter called Maria Nagaya. Not long before he died, Ivan divorced Maria Nagaya in order to marry Lady Mary Hastings, a lady-in-waiting to Queen Elizabeth of England.

At the age of fifty-three, Ivan began to suffer from a strange disease — a rotting of his internal organs. The illness spread and he died on 18 March 1584. Although chiefly known as a tyrant, Ivan IV was one of the best educated men of his time. He had an excellent memory and a good knowledge of theology. Besides his letters to Prince Kurbsky, he also composed music, the text of the church service in honour of Our Lady of Vladimir and the canon to the Archangel Michael. He printed the first Russian books in Moscow and built St Basil's Church on Red Square.

Metropolitan Initiating Ivan the Terrible into the Schema before his Death. Artist: Pyotr Geller

Tsar
Fedor I
1557–1598

Parents:
Tsar **Ivan IV Vasilyevich the Terrible** (1530–1584) and Tsarina **Anastasia Romanovna Zakharina-Yurieva** (?–1560).

Wife:
Irina Fedorovna Godunova (1557–1604), sister of Boris Godunov. Married: 1580.

Children:
Feodosia (1592–1593).

Fedor I was born in Moscow on 31 May 1557. A contemporary described him as "short, squat and fattish, with a weak constitution inclined to dropsy. He has a hooked nose and unsteady gait resulting from a weakness of the limbs. He is overweight and inactive, but always smiles, almost laughing ... Although simple and weak-minded, he is always kind and pleasant in conversation, quiet and gracious. Not aggressive or a plotter, he is extremely superstitious."

Fedor was crowned tsar on 31 May 1584. The coronation ceremony was performed by Metropolitan Dionysius, who dressed him in the royal regalia and handed him the sceptre with the words: "Treasure the gonfalons of great Russia."

Everyone in the cathedral, however, knew that Fedor was incapable of ruling by himself. A fierce battle soon broke out among the boyars for influence over the new tsar.

The power struggle was won by the tsar's brother-in-law, Boris Godunov, who became the *de facto* ruler of the country. Fedor was married to Boris's sister Irina. In 1592, they had a daughter called Feodosia, who died a year later. There was a rumour that Irina had given birth to a son, whom her brother substituted for a girl, to ensure that there were no heirs to the throne.

Fedor led a modest and moderate lifestyle, piously attending church services, visiting monasteries and holding long conversations with artisans and icon-painters. He watched with interest bear fights and fist fights, although he did not receive much pleasure from them. Mundane affairs were of little interest to the tsar, whose thoughts were concentrated on higher things.

Tsar Fedor I, Patriarch Job
and Boris Godunov

1584	Founding of Archangel. Death of Yermak.
1586	Founding of Tobolsk.
1589	Establishment of the patriarchate.
1590	Founding of Saratov and Tsaritsyn.
1590–93	War with Sweden ending with the return of the towns lost in 1583.
1591	Death of Tsarevich Dmitry.
1593	Founding of Berezov.
1595	Founding of Obdorsk.
1597	Law on the capture and registration of runaway peasants.
1598	Final conquest of Siberia.
	Death of Tsar Fedor and the end of the Rurikid dynasty.

The most important event during the reign of Tsar Fedor was the election of Metropolitan Job as patriarch of Russia in 1589. Job was the first ever independent patriarch of the Russian Orthodox Church. He was originally called Ioann and brought up at the Monastery of the Dormition in the town of Staritsa. He took the habit between 1552 and 1555 and was promoted to the rank of archimandrite after Ivan the Terrible visited the monastery around 1569. Soon after this, he was transferred to Moscow. Between 1571 and 1580, he was the abbot of first St Simon's Monastery and then the Novospassky Monastery. Job's ascetic lifestyle and expert knowledge of the scriptures and liturgical books led to his promotion to the post of bishop. In December 1586, he was appointed metropolitan of Russia, in place of Dionysius.

In 1588, the eastern patriarchs decided to found a patriarchate in Russia, elevating the Russian Orthodox Church to an independent and equal standing with the other national churches. Job was elected to the post on 23 January 1589 and ordained on 26 January. In 1591, he headed the official enquiry into the death of Tsarevich Dmitry in Uglich. After consulting with the church council and the duma of boyars, the patriarch announced his verdict — the tsarevich had accidentally stabbed himself and not been murdered.

After the death of Tsar Fedor I and the refusal of his wife, Irina Godunova, to accept the throne, Patriarch Job became the head of state in 1598. As he was much obliged

Tsar Fedor I Making Boris Godunov
the Ruler of Russia

blessing. He then returned to Staritsa, where he died on 19 June 1607. He was buried at the Monastery of the Dormition. In 1652, his remains were transferred to the Dormition Cathedral in the Moscow Kremlin. The acts of Patriarch Job include the foundation of the Don Monastery in Moscow in 1591 and the sending of missionaries to the Volga region, Siberia and the Far North. In 1990, he was canonised by the Russian Orthodox Church. In 1586, the foundry man Andrei Chokhov (Chekhov) cast the world's largest cannon in Moscow. The Tsar Cannon stands on an enormous gun carriage cast in 1835. Andrei Chokhov created over twenty cannons, each of which had its own name — the Bear Cannon, Wolf Cannon, Fox Cannon or Achilles Cannon. He also designed a multi-barrel cannon and a gun with a special wedge-shaped breech mechanism. As Tsar Fedor I was incapable of ruling on his own, a council of regents was created, consisting of Bogdan Belsky, Nikita Yuriev and Prince Ivan Mstislavsky. Each council member had his own personal interests and influenced government

Patriarch Job of Moscow.
Parsuna

Cupolas of the Higher Cathedral of the Saviour
in the Moscow Kremlin

to Boris Godunov for his promotion to the post of patriarch, Job offered the former's candidature as tsar to the Land Council. On 21 February 1598, he led a religious procession to Boris Godunov, imploring him to accept the throne.

When False Dmitry I appeared, Patriarch Job denounced the pretender. He declared that the person claiming to be Tsarevich Dmitry was in fact an heretic and defrocked monk, Grishka Otrepiev, and the tsarevich had really died.

After the death of Boris Godunov, Job supported his son Fedor. When the royal family was overthrown by forces loyal to False Dmitry I in June 1605, the patriarch was arrested during a service at the Dormition Cathedral. He was driven on a rough cart to the Monastery of the Dormition in Staritsa, where he was blinded, while his house was ransacked. Job was succeeded by Archbishop Ignatius of Ryazan and only returned to Moscow following the murder of False Dmitry I, the imprisonment of Patriarch Ignatius at the Monastery of the Miracle and the accession of Basil Shuisky. On 20 February 1607, he reappeared at the Dormition Cathedral, where he forgave the people of Moscow and gave them his

In 1586, the foundry man Andrei Chokhov cast the world's largest cannon in Moscow. The barrel was over seventeen feet long, weighed an impressive forty tons and had an incredible calibre of thirty-five inches. The weapon was originally created with the purpose of defending the Kremlin. It was called the Tsar Cannon as the bronze barrel bore a relief of Fedor I. The canon was never actually fired and has remained on display in the Kremlin ever since.

Russian Embassy Bearing Gifts to Holy Roman Emperor Maximilian II
at the Imperial Diet in Regensburg. 1576. Engraving

were sent abroad to study foreign languages. In 1586, the king of Kakheti (now part of eastern Georgia) appealed to Russia for protection, but the country was still not strong enough to offer any real assistance. A series of fortifications were built in the south of Russia to repel the attacks of Khan Kaza-Girei and the Crimean Tatars. The peace treaty with the Polish-Lithuanian Commonwealth was renewed in 1587. After a war with Sweden (1590–93), lands lost by Ivan the Terrible were returned to Russia under the terms of the Treaty of Täyssinä (1595). All these and other events took place during the reign of the "good fool in God," as Fedor I was known by his subjects. The tsar's personality evoked the interest

Moscow Kremlin. Chalice and Censer.
1580s. Donated by Irina Godunova

policy in his own way. Bogdan Belsky was the nephew of Malyuta Skuratov, the former right-hand man of Ivan the Terrible. Belsky attempted to capture power for himself and restore the *oprichnina* system. In 1584, a popular uprising broke out in Moscow against Belsky, banishing this energetic and ambitious man from the capital.

Boris Godunov, a former member of the *oprichniki*, had enormous influence over Fedor. Descended from an old family of boyars, he was the son-in-law of Malyuta Skuratov and the brother-in-law of the tsar. Boris Godunov gradually ousted all his rivals — Prince Ivan Mstislavsky was forced into a monastery, Nikita Yuriev died and Prince Ivan Shuisky fell into disfavour and was killed. This left Godunov as the *de facto* tsar of Russia. The word "ruler" was included in his boyar title and he entered into personal correspondence with foreign kings and queens, who referred to him as "prince" or "lord protector."

Boris Godunov expanded Russian trade with Britain, Holland and the rest of Western Europe through the northern port of Archangel. Foreign experts were invited to work and teach in Russia, while young Russian noblemen

Moscow Kremlin. Tsar Cannon. 1586.
Master: Andrei Chokhov

After the death of Ivan the Terrible, his youngest son Dmitry lived with his mother, Maria Nagaya, in the town of Uglich in Yaroslavl Province. In May 1591, he was found with his throat cut in the palace courtyard. Although the official version claimed that Dmitry had fallen on a knife during an epileptic fit, popular suspicion fell on Boris Godunov, as Dmitry's death cleared his path to the throne. Historians, however, reject these rumours.

Murder of Tsarevich Dmitry.
Fresco of the Church
of Dmitry-on-Blood. Uglich

Uglich.
Chambers of Tsarevich Dmitry

Bell Announcing the Death
of Tsarevich Dmitry. Uglich.
Church of Dmitry-on-Blood

Murder of Tsarevich Dmitry.
Artist: Alexander Moravov

of both contemporaries and future generations. In 1868, Alexei Tolstoy published his tragedy *Tsar Fedor Ioannovich*, which is still widely performed to this day in Russia. The writer described the concept of the play to theatrical directors: "Not departing from the traditional story, merely filling in the gaps, I have allowed myself to depict Fedor not simply as a week-willed and meek ascetic, but someone naturally endowed with great mental qualities, despite a certain dullness of mind and the complete absence of any will. His innate inability to act was increased by his father's oppression and the constant fear in which he lived until the age of twenty-seven, when Tsar Ivan died.

"Fedor's kindness exceeded all normal bounds. It was so great that it could sometimes reach the point when feelings and thoughts, constituting separate attributes on the lower levels, come together and mix in an indissoluble knowledge of the truth. Notwithstanding his mental limitations, Fedor was therefore often capable of holding views no less wise than those of Boris Godunov. In the scene of the report on the boyars who have fled to Lithuania, both come to the same conclusion — Godunov through the mind and Fedor through the heart. Fedor was not always capable, however, of replacing the mind with the heart.

In 1571, Boris Godunov was the best man at the wedding of Ivan the Terrible and Martha Vasilyevna Sobakina. Two weeks later, Tsarina Martha died "with her virginity still intact." This event inspired Nikolai Rimsky-Korsakov's opera *The Tsar's Bride*, based on a drama by Lev Mey.

In normal circumstances, this talent was eclipsed by certain shortcomings, closely linked to his weakness of character. He did not like, for example, to confess to others or to himself that he was weak. This often led to inappropriate — though generally short-lived — stubbornness.

"He sometimes wanted to show that he was independent and nothing flattered him more than accusations of inflexibility or severity. He was a great busybody in everything that did not concern affairs of state. In his opinion, no one knew the human heart better than he did. The reconciliation of enemies was not only a duty, but a great delight. Although piety was part and parcel of his natural disposition, it verged on asceticism, as a result of his early protest against the depravity and harshness of his father. Asceticism subsequently became a habit, though he was never a pedant. He did not regard secular festivities as a sin;

Boris Godunov and Tsarina Martha.
Artist: Nikolai Ge

he enjoyed bear baiting and did not regard mummer shows as serving the devil. Like all timid people, he had great admiration for courage. The heroic character of Prince Shuisky and the daring of the merchant Krasilnikov tugged at his heart strings.

"Fedor's magnanimity knew no bounds. Personal insults could not touch him, though any insult to someone else was capable of making him forget his usual meekness. If the insult concerned someone he especially liked, his indignation made him lose his self-control. He shouted and fumed, seeing nothing but the delivered injustice. In doing so, he hastened to make good use of this mood. Knowing that he did not have long to live, he was quick to issue strict orders — justified in his mind, yet not in keeping with his character.

"When Fedor succeeded to the throne, he was in no doubt about his own inability and gave

Sister Martha, Basil Shuisky and the Patriarch Confirming the Death of Tsarevich Dmitry

Godunov *carte blanche*, not intending to interfere in anything himself. But Godunov did not count on initially taking full responsibility. He found it useful to hide behind the authority of Fedor. He maintained the outward show of an unlimited sovereign, reporting everything to Fedor and asking his advice on all matters.

"Fedor gradually, with the assistance of the inevitable court flatterers, convinced himself that he was not as incapable as he had thought. Tragedy, however, overtook him. His natural laziness and dislike for governing continued to distance him from affairs of state, yet he was already accustomed to thinking that Godunov was acting in accordance with his own instructions. Only during major crises, when Godunov's will directly contradicted Fedor's clemency, like when Godunov threatened to abandon him if he did not give up Basil Shuisky, did Fedor's self-delusions vanish. He understood Godunov's independent power and, incapable of opposing him as tsar, reproached him as a human being and a Christian."

Fedor I died in Moscow on 7 January 1598. He was remembered chiefly for his piety and politeness. After his death, Irina Godunova was offered the throne, but she refused. On the ninth day after her husband's death, she entered a convent as Sister Alexandra. The only other lawful claimant to the throne was Martha (Maria), daughter of Ivan the Terrible's cousin, Vladimir Staritsky, and the widow of King Magnus of Livonia. When she returned to Russia, she was forced to enter a nunnery. Her daughter Eudokia died in suspicious circumstances, thus ending the Rurikid dynasty.

ГРАЖДАНИНУ МИНИНУ И КНЯЗЮ ПОЖАРСКОМУ
БЛАГОДАРНАЯ РОССІЯ. ЛѢТА 1818

THE TIME OF TROUBLES. INTERREGNUM

1598–1613

The period between the death of the last tsar of the Rurikid dynasty and the accession of the first tsar of the Romanov dynasty were years of civil war in Russian history. This fifteen-year period of confusion affected all classes of Russian society and all aspects of Russian life — the economy, government, domestic and foreign policy, ideology and morale. The Time of Troubles began with a three-year famine during the reign of Boris Godunov. The lack of food led to a wave of popular discontent and mass protests, which was exploited by Russia's neighbours — Poland, Sweden, Crimea and Turkey. Polish and Swedish armies invaded Russian and captured several towns. False Dmitry I sacked Moscow at the head of a Polish army. The country was on the verge of ruin.

The Russian people rallied, however, liberating Moscow and expelling the foreign invaders. The Land Council convened to elect a new tsar. As the people set about restoring their ruined economy, state and lives, Russia rose again from the ashes.

Tsar
Boris Godunov
1552–1605

Descendant of a Tatar *murza* Chet who adopted the Orthodox faith

Wife:

Maria Grigoryevna Skuratova-Belskaya (?–1605), daughter of Grigory Lukianovitch (Malyuta) Skuratov-Belsky. Married in 1571/72.

Children:
Fedor (see Fedor).
Xenia (1582–1622).

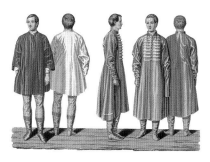

Seventeenth-Century Clothes of Boyars.
Artist: Fedor Solntsev

Boris Godunov was descended from a Tatar who had abandoned the Golden Horde during the reign of Ivan Kalita. He took the Christian name of Zacharius and founded the Ipatiev Monastery in the outskirts of Kostroma (named after St Hypatius Gangrsky). In Russia, the Saburov and Godunov families both traced their ancestry from Zacharius.

Plan of the Moscow Kremlin.
Early 17th century. Detail

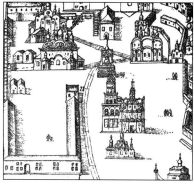

Boris Godunov began his career in the *oprichnina* after marrying the daughter of the tsar's (Ivan the Terrible) confidant, Malyuta Skuratov. In September 1580, Godunov became a boyar and eventually one of the closest associates of Ivan the Terrible. He amassed a large fortune and during the reign of Ivan's son, Fedor I, was the *de facto* ruler of Russia. Boris Godunov had two children — a son called Fedor and a daughter called Xenia. Fedor was an intelligent young man who received an excellent education from foreign tutors. From an early age, his father prepared him for the throne.

When Fedor I died without leaving any heirs, the government of the country automatically passed to Patriarch Job. The head of the Russian church believed that Boris Godunov should become tsar, on the strength of his success during the reign of Fedor I.

When the official period of mourning came to an end, a council of 474 people was convened on 17 February 1598. After spending five days discussing Boris's candidature, the council offered him the crown on 21 February. The coronation was held at the Dormition Cathedral on 1 September (Russia still followed the Julian calendar and 1 September was New Year's Day).

1598	The irregular army of the nobility forestalls an invasion by Khan Kaza-Girei and the Crimean Tatars.
1600	The Romanov family is accused of plotting against Boris Godunov and banished.
1601–04	Famine leads to mass deaths, epidemics and a wave of public disorders.
1602	False Dmitry I surfaces in Poland, claiming to be the son of Ivan the Terrible.
1603	Freedom is granted to all menial servants whose owners refuse to feed them during the famine.
	Uprising of peasants and menial servants led by Ataman Khlopko.
1604	False Dmitry I and two thousand Polish mercenaries invade Russia.
	Foundation of Tomsk.
January 1605	Defeat of False Dmitry I at the Battle of Dobrynichi.

Boris Godunov with Ivan the Terrible.
Artist: Ilya Repin

Boris Godunov did all he could to strengthen the Russian state. The foundation of the patriarchate reflected the growing prestige of the nation. After the death of Tsar Fedor I in 1598, the Land Council showed its appreciation by offering the throne to Boris Godunov.

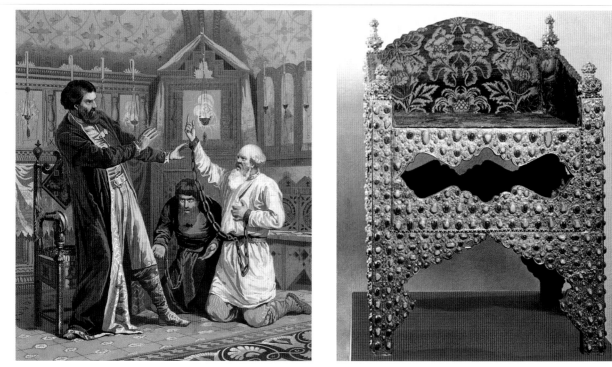

Boris Godunov and Magicians Showing his Reign.
Artist: Alexei Kivshenko

Throne of Boris Godunov.
Moscow Armoury

Novodevichy Convent.
Founded in 1524. It was here that Boris Godunov was declared tsar.

Boris Godunov was a shrewd and clever politician. He centralised state power, relying on the support of the nobility. In order to ingratiate himself with the common people, he made several handsome gestures. Rural inhabitants did not have to pay any taxes for a whole year. Merchants were freed of paying customs for two years, while public servants received an additional year's salary. Boris Godunov was an energetic, ambitious and talented statesman. He continued the policies of Ivan the Terrible, expanding Russian control over Siberia and the Caucasus. The tsar built new fortifications to defend Moscow — White Town and Earth Town — and Russia's frontiers. Boris Godunov did all he could to strengthen the Russian state. Godunov built new towns, fortresses and churches and invited foreign

Boris Godunov was an energetic, ambitious and talented statesman. He continued the policies of Ivan the Terrible, expanding Russian control over Siberia and the Caucasus. The tsar built new fortifications to defend Moscow — White Town and Earth Town — and Russia's frontiers.

Portrait of Fedor Chaliapin as Boris Godunov in Modest Mussorgsky's Opera *Boris Godunov*. Artist: Alexander Golovin

experts to come and work in Russia. He even wanted to open a school in Moscow run by foreigners, but ran up against the opposition of the church. In 1600, the Ivan Bell Tower inside the Kremlin was put up above the existing church of St John (Ivan) Climacus. At a height of 260 feet, it was the tallest building in Moscow. The words "king of glory" were emblazoned on the cross and the tower was popularly known as "Ivan the Great." Godunov was famous for his lavish banquets. One feast in the town of Serpukhov lasted six weeks; another was held for half a million troops. The food was served on gold and silver plates, while the beverages were poured into silver goblets. The tables literally groaned under the weight of the dishes. Wine and vodka were kept in special silver barrels, while beer was served from silver basins. Guests were presented with rich fabrics — velvet, brocade and silk.

News of the high quality of Russian vodka spread outside Russia and Shah Abbas of Persia asked Boris Godunov to send him a distillery. In September 1600, Russian envoys set sail for Persia, carrying "two goblets, pipes, lids and trivets" and "two hundred buckets of wines." The shah never received his vodka distillery — five miles before Saratov, the envoys ran into a storm and their ship sank.

Boris Godunov was equally cunning in his foreign policy. Taking advantage of domestic problems in Sweden in 1595, he forced the Swedes to sign a treaty returning lands lost during the long Livonian War.

Although Boris Godunov had been elected tsar of Russia by the Land Council, after the death of Tsar Fedor I in 1598, the boyars still regarded him as a low-born upstart.

Boris Godunov had two children — a son called Fedor and a daughter called Xenia. Fedor was an intelligent young man who received an excellent education from foreign tutors. From an early age, his father prepared him for the throne. Famed for her beauty, Xenia was also well educated.

Boris Godunov Examining a Map Used to Teach his Son.
Artist: N. Nekrasov

Tsar Boris Godunov and his Children Fedor and Xenia.
Artist: Alexei Kivshenko

Palace of Boris Godunov in the Kremlin (?).
Engraving by Peter Picart. Detail

Members of the Romanov, Shuisky and Mstislavsky families believed that they had more right to sit on the throne. They supported the rumours that Tsarevich Dmitry was alive and on his way to Moscow to demand his father's crown. In 1601 and 1602, the harvests failed and famine swept the country, followed by a wave of epidemics. Over 127,000 people died in Moscow alone. The price of bread increased one hundred times and there were reports of cannibalism. Although the duma of boyars was summoned in 1603, nothing could be done to solve the problems. People began to murmur that the troubles were an affliction sent by God to punish Russia for illegally electing Boris Godunov as tsar.

Boris Godunov built an unprecedented number of new towns and churches. In 1600, the Ivan Bell Tower inside the Kremlin was extended. At a height of 260 feet, it was the tallest building in Moscow. The words "king of glory" were emblazoned on the cross and the tower was popularly known as "Ivan the Great."

Ivan the Great Bell Tower in the Moscow Kremlin.
16th to 17th centuries

A series of popular uprisings broke out, the largest of which was led by Khlopko in 1603. In October 1604, a defrocked monk called Grishka Otrepiev claimed that he was really the son of Ivan the Terrible, Tsarevich Dmitry, and invaded the country with a Polish army. Although government forces under the command of Basil Shuisky managed to defeat the pretender in January 1605, he escaped to Putivl and rumours of the tsarevich's survival continued to sweep Moscow. Boris Godunov died of gout in Moscow on 23 April 1605, although it was rumoured that he had poisoned himself in a fit of despair. He was buried inside the Kremlin, in the Archangel Cathedral.

Tsar
Fedor Godunov
1589–1605

Parents:

Tsar **Boris Godunov** (1552–1605)
and Tsarina **Maria Grigoryevna
Skuratova-Belskaya** (?–1605).

Fedor Godunov was the son of Boris Godunov. An intelligent and cultivated youth, he became tsar at the age of sixteen, during one of the most difficult periods in Russian history. Besides Fedor and Xenia, Boris Godunov had another son — his first-born. The boy once fell ill and the doctors were powerless to help him. Boris Godunov prayed in vain for the health of his son, attending churches and visiting holy places. Desperate, he ordered him to be given "holy" water and took him to St Basil's Cathedral in a hard frost, resulting in the death of his son and heir. Fedor Godunov received a first-class education. His father wanted to marry him to a foreign princess and held ultimately unsuccessful negotiations with Queen Elizabeth I of England. When agreeing the Russo-Norwegian border with Denmark, the tsar proposed that his daughter should marry the crown prince. Prince John, the brother of King Christian IV, came to Moscow, but fell ill and died in October 1602. In 1605, proposals for a marriage between Xenia and the duke of Schleswig were interrupted by the death of Boris Godunov.

He ruled the country for a total of fifty days. When Muscovites were kissing the cross and taking their oath to the new tsar, Grishka Otrepiev was already moving towards the capital with his army.

The False Dmitry I — as Grishka Otrepiev was known, to distinguish him from a second pretender, False

50

Fedor Godunov was too young to overcome circumstances and take the control of the state into his own hands. No important events took place during the reign of Fedor Godunov, which only lasted fifty days, until he was overthrown by the supporters of False Dmitry I.

Last Minutes of the Godunovs.
Artists: Stadler and Pattitot

Agents of Dmitry the Pretender Killing
the Son of Boris Godunov. Artist: Konstantin Makovsky

Dmitry II — sent a proclamation to his supporters in Moscow, promising to reward those who recognised him as the rightful tsar and to kill those who did not. The people of Moscow were thrown into confusion, with many believing that he was indeed the son of Ivan the Terrible. A mob broke into the Kremlin, ransacked the palace and arrested Boris Godunov's widow and children.

On 3 June 1605, the royal family was overthrown by a group of boyars led by Basil Shuisky and Basil Mosalsky. Hired assassins overthrew Patriarch Job and strangled Fedor Godunov and his mother. Their bodies were shown to the people, who were told that they had taken poison.

Several days later, Boris Godunov's coffin was removed from the Archangel Cathedral and reburied at the more humble Barsonofiev Monastery near the Lubyanka. The people were told that he too had taken poison. The bodies of his widow and son, who were said to have committed suicide, were buried alongside him without a funeral service.

Although Boris Godunov's daughter Xenia survived, she was forced to become the concubine of False Dmitry I. When he tired of her, she entered a nunnery under the name of Olga. The seven-year reign of the Godunov dynasty had come to an end.

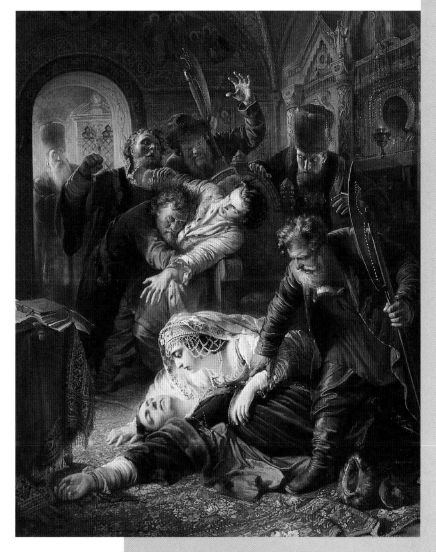

Tsar
False Dmitry I
?–1606

When the government of Boris Godunov learnt that someone claiming to be the Tsarevich Dmitry had surfaced in Poland, they immediately launched an investigation and published the findings. The pretender's real name was Yury Otrepiev, the son of a Streltsy centurion who had worked as a menial servant in Moscow, first with the Romanov family and then with Prince Boris Cherkassky. He later became a monk under the name of Grigory or "Grishka" for short. Grishka served at the Monastery of the Miracle in Moscow, where Patriarch Job promoted him to the post of deacon. After making lewd statements, the brotherhood wanted to exile him to the Solovki Monastery in northern Russia, but he escaped to Poland, where he claimed to be the son of Ivan the Terrible. He was received by King Sigismund III, who granted him an annual allowance of five thousand roubles. The former monk assembled an army with the intention of marching on Moscow and seizing the throne. Grishka Otrepiev's plan succeeded brilliantly. He entered the Russian capital on 20 June 1605 and was crowned by the new patriarch, Ignatius, in the Dormition Cathedral on 21 July. His wife Maryna was crowned empress on 8 May and spent the following week in celebrations. On 16 May, Grishka and Maryna were awoken by a ringing of bells, shouts and gunfire. Men hired by Basil Shuisky broke into their bedroom, murdered the False Dmitry and raped his wife. The mob was eventually dispersed by boyars, who confiscated all the money, jewels and other property appropriated by Maryna and her father. The deposed empress and her relatives were marched to the Polish border. Before they reached there, however, they were intercepted by the envoys of a second pretender, False Dmitry II, who had set up camp at Tushino near Moscow (earning him the popular title of the "thief of Tushino"). He offered to restore Maryna to the throne if she would identify him as False Dmitry I, who had

Grishka's army was headed by a Polish magnate called Jerzy Mniszech. One day, Otrepiev fell in love with his daughter Maryna and asked her to marry him. A handsome woman with many admirers, Maryna was not enthralled by the defrocked monk, whose face was disfigured by two enormous warts. Her father, however, explained the benefits that could result from such a marriage if Otrepiev managed to seize the Russian throne.

survived the events of 16 May. She agreed to his plan and, when his army arrived, flung her arms around his neck and passionately kissed her "husband". The attempt of the False Dmitry II to usurp the Russian throne was equally ill-fated. Before he could march on Moscow, his nerves gave way and he fled to Kaluga, abandoning Maryna and his army. His wife's letters complaining of physical abuse by his soldiers went unanswered. Dressed in a Hussars uniform, Maryna went to Kaluga herself in search of her husband. Sensing that nothing good would come of their attempt to seize the throne, his associates tired of the pretender and decided to get rid of him. On 10 December 1610, when they were out hunting, Peter Urusov beheaded False Dmitry II and hacked his body into little pieces. Maryna learnt of her second husband's murder when she was in her final month of pregnancy.

During his brief reign as tsar of Moscow (1605–06), False Dmitry I attempted to bring the rulers of France, Germany, Venice and Poland together in an anti-Turkish alliance. The Pope, the Jesuits and King Sigismund of Poland all planned to manipulate the pretender, but they misjudged him. The former monk refused to introduce Roman Catholicism or the Jesuits into Russia. When Maryna arrived in Russia, he made her attend the Orthodox Church. Although personally indifferent to religion, the False Dmitry I wanted to avoid angering the people. He also refused to make any territorial concessions or financial payments to Poland. Upholders of traditional values did not like some of the concessions introduced by False Dmitry I following the arrival of Maryna Mniszech in Moscow. Others disliked his clear preference for foreigners. The common people took to him, however, and attacked anyone claiming that he had usurped the throne. He was only overthrown by a plot hatched by boyars led by Basil Shuisky.

Maryna Mniszech
Polish wife of False Dmitry I

Last Minutes of Dmitry the Pretender.
Artist: Carl von Wenig

Gathering up what was left of his body, she brought the remains back to Kaluga in a sledge. His murder was avenged by one of her own commanders, Ivan Zarutsky from Ternopole. Several days later, Maryna gave birth to a son, whom she called Ivan. She married Zarutsky and they proceeded to ride across the country, robbing Russian towns. After the succession of Michael Romanov, the couple fled to Astrachan. They planned to raise a fresh army to march on Moscow, but were betrayed to the Streltsy guards. Maryna's second entry into the Russian capital, eight years after the first, was less triumphant. Her son was hung and her husband was impaled. Maryna's own fate is not clear; she was either drowned or died in prison in 1614.

Tsar
Basil IV Ivanovich Shuisky
1552–1612

Son of an unknown woman and **Ivan Andreyevich Shuisky** (1533–1673), a boyar descended from Andrei of Suzdal, the third son of St Alexander Nevsky.

Wives:

Princess **Elena Mikhailovna Repnina.**

Princess **Ekaterina (Elena) Petrovna Buinosova-Rostovskaya** (?–1626). Married on 17 January 1608.

His second wife, who became Tsarina Maria, bore him two daughters, Anna and Anastasia, who both died in infancy. When he was overthrown, he was separated from his wife. She was forced into a nunnery as Sister Helen and died in 1626.

Prince Basil Ivanovich Shuisky came from an old branch of the Suzdal princes descended from Rurik. Becoming a boyar in 1584, he headed the unsuccessful opposition to Boris Godunov in 1587. After falling into disfavour, he managed to win back the tsar's trust and was forgiven. In May 1591, Shuisky headed the committee of investigation into the death of Tsarevich Dmitry in Uglich. The commission came to the conclusion that the tsarevich had died naturally, as a result of illness. Basil Shuisky took part in the campaign against the False Dmitry I (1604–05). After the death of Boris Godunov, however, he crossed sides and joined the pretender. On two occasions, Shuisky headed a plot against False Dmitry I. The first time he was sentenced to death, but forgiven. The second plot ended in the False Dmitry's murder on 17 May 1606. (After burning the pretender's body, the boyars placed the ashes in a cannon and fired them in the direction of Poland.) Two days later, on 19 May, a crowd gathered and proclaimed Basil Shuisky the new tsar — without a council or reference to representatives of the people. Ascending the throne, Basil Shuisky swore on the cross to preserve the privileges of the boyars and not to pass sentence on any of them without calling the duma of boyars. Patriarch Ignatius, who had been elected by False Dmitry I, was

...... 1606-1607

Ivan Bolotnikov led a popular uprising in the south of Russia and besieged Moscow in October 1606. Two months later, he was forced to retreat to Kaluga and surrounded, but then he escaped to Tula, where he was besieged by the forces of Basil Shuisky. The tsar blocked off the River Ula and flooded the town. The insurgents opened the city gates and were defeated. Ivan Bolotnikov was blinded and thrown down a shaft.

Uprising led by Ivan Bolotnikov.
Artist: Ernst Lissner

1606–07	Uprising led by Ivan Bolotnikov.
1608–09	False Dmitry II sets up camp at Tushino outside Moscow.
1608–10	Polish forces besiege the St Sergius Monastery of the Trinity.
	Alliance with Sweden.
1609	Polish and Swedish intervention.
1609–11	King Sigismund III of Poland besieges Smolensk.
1610	Basil Shuisky was overthrown by a group of boyars led by Prince Fedor Mstislavsky. He was replaced by a new government of seven boyars, known as the *semiboyarschina*.

overthrown by the new tsar and imprisoned at the Monastery of the Miracle. Russia remained without a patriarch. Basil was crowned by Metropolitan Isidor of Novgorod on 1 June 1606. The fifty-four year-old tsar was a puny man with poor eyesight and a stoop. Cunning and mean, he believed in magic and relied on a web of informers. Shortly after Shuisky's coronation, a second pretender called Dmitry emerged, also claiming to be the son of Ivan the Terrible.

Ivan Bolotnikov led a popular uprising in support of False Dmitry II in the south of Russia in autumn 1606. When his forces attempted to march on Moscow, they were defeated by government troops near the village of Kotly in December 1606 and finally routed in autumn 1607.

The False Dmitry II began his own march on Moscow in August 1607. In the spring of 1608, his troops besieged Moscow from their headquarters in Tushino.

In an attempt to defeat the False Dmitry II, Basil Shuisky signed an alliance with Sweden in February 1608. Sweden agreed to help the tsar in return for territorial concessions. In spring 1609, fifteen thousand Swedish troops entered Russia from the north, while Poland took advantage of the situation by invading Russia from the west. With the Polish army at the gates of

Overthrow of the Pretender.
Artist: N. Nekrasov

Ascending the throne, Basil Shuisky swore on the cross to preserve the privileges of the boyars and not to pass sentence on any of them without the calling the duma of boyars. Patriarch Ignatius, who had been elected by False Dmitry I, was overthrown by the new tsar and imprisoned at the Monastery of the Miracle. Russia remained without a patriarch.

Shuisky and Delagardi Entering Moscow.
Artist: Vyacheslav Schwartz

King Sigismund III
of Poland

Moscow in July 1610, a group of boyars led by Prince Fedor Mstislavsky overthrew Shuisky and forced him to become a monk. He and his family were then sent to Poland as prisoners. Shuisky was replaced by a new government of seven boyars, known as the *semiboyarschina*. In August 1610, they agreed to recognise Prince Wladyslaw, son of King Sigismund of Poland, as tsar of Russia. Under the command of Hetman Stanislaus Zolkiewski, the Poles captured and looted Moscow. Zolkiewski demanded that the boyars recognise Prince Wladyslaw of Poland as the tsar of Russia. The boyars consented, on condition that Wladyslaw convert to Orthodoxy. The Poles agreed, but failed to keep their promise. The Polish army entered the Kremlin and the boyars swore an oath of allegiance to Wladyslaw on 27 August 1610. This was an enormous betrayal of the national interests. Polish soldiers ransacked the country, robbing and killing the population. Smolensk and other west Russian towns were annexed by Poland, while Swedish forces occupied Novgorod. The reign of Basil Shuisky ended in the bankruptcy and foreign occupation of Russia.

Kuzma Minin, the burgomaster of Nizhny Novgorod, responded by forming a popular militia in autumn 1611. Funds were collected and an army of national

While Basil Shuisky was besieging Tula, a new pretender appeared. False Dmitry II advanced towards Moscow in summer 1608 and set up camp at Tushino, earning him the nickname of the "thief of Tushino". The pretender besieged Moscow for twenty-one months.

False Dmitry II
("Thief of Tushino")

liberation was created, headed by Kuzma Minin and Prince Dmitry Pozharsky. The Russian nation rallied in the face of the foreign aggression. The Poles were expelled from Moscow in October 1612 by the volunteer militia led by Prince Dmitry Pozharsky and citizen Kuzma Minin and a Cossack army led by Prince Trubetskoi. On 22 October 1612, the feast day of the icon of the Mother of God of Kazan, the Russian militia captured Kitai-Gorod (Chinatown). Four days later, the Polish garrison in the Kremlin

Kuzma Minin's Appeal.
Artist: Konstantin Makovsky

Citizen Kuzma Minin and Prince Dmitry Pozharsky.
Artist: Mikhail Scotti

surrendered. In memory of the liberation of Moscow, Prince Pozharsky built the Church of the Mother of God of Kazan on Red Square. (In 1818, a monument to Minin and Pozharsky by sculptor Ivan Martos was opened in front of St Basil's Cathedral.) In November 1612, Basil Shuisky died in Warsaw. In 1635, his ashes were returned to Russia, along with an indemnity of sables worth 3,674 roubles. The remains of Basil and his family were buried in the Archangel Cathedral of the Moscow Kremlin. The Land Council met in Moscow in 1613 and offered the throne to the sixteen-year-old Michael Romanov.

THE SECOND RUSSIAN DYNASTY. THE ROMANOVS

1613–1918

Russia slowly rose from the ruins, returned to a normal life and restored its statehood. On 21 February 1613, representatives of different classes gathered at the Dormition Cathedral in the Moscow Kremlin to elect a new tsar. They unanimously voted for Michael Fedorovich Romanov — the member of an old Russian family descended from Andrei Ivanovich Kobyla, a boyar of Prince Ivan Kalita. Andrei Kobyla inherited his unusual surname ("mare") from his father, Prince Glanda-Kambila Divonovich of Prussia, who moved to Russia in the thirteenth century and converted to Orthodox in 1287. Two of Andrei's children also had names associated with animals — Semyon Zherebets ("Stud") and Fedor Koshka ("Cat"). Fedor Koshka was the head of the Koshkin family. His grandson, Yury Zakharovich, had the surname of Koshkin-Zakharin, while his great-grandson Michael had the surname Zakharin-Yuriev. Michael's grandson, Nikita Romanovich, became known as Zakharin-Romanov, while Nikita's son Fedor was simply Romanov — like all subsequent members of the family. The Romanov dynasty ruled Russia until 1917.

Tsar
Michael Fedorovich
1596–1645

Parents:
Boyar **Fedor Nikitovich Romanov** (1553–1633) and **Xenia Ivanovna Shestova** (?–1631), from a family of nobles in Mozhaisk.

Wives:
Maria Vladimirovna Dolgorukova, daughter of Prince Vladimir Dolgorukov. Married on 19 September 1624.
Eudokia Lukianovna Streshneva (1608–1645). Married on 5 February 1626.

Children of Tsar Michael and Eudokia Streshneva:
Irina was born in Moscow on 22 April 1627. She lived in Moscow and the village of Rubtsovo, which she inherited from her paternal grandmother.
She enjoyed landscape gardening.
On 29 June 1672, she served as godmother to her nephew, the future Peter the Great. Never married. Died in Moscow on 8 February 1679.
Pelageya was born in Moscow on 20 April 1628 and baptised by Patriarch Filaret in the Monastery of the Miracle.
Died in Moscow on 25 November 1629.
Alexei (see Alexis).
Anna was born in Moscow on 14 July 1630. Never married. Entered a convent as Sister Anphisa. Died in Moscow in 1692.
Martha (1631–1632).
Ioann (1633–1639).
Sophia (1634–1636).
Tatyana was born in Moscow on 5 January 1636. Served as godmother to Tsarevna Martha Alexeyevna, Tsarevna Maria Ioannovna, Tsarevna Feodosia Ioannovna and Tsarevich Alexei (son of Peter the Great). Died in Moscow on 24 August 1706.
Eudokia was born and died in Moscow on 10 February 1637.
Vasily was born and died in Moscow on 25 March 1639.

After the death of Tsar Fedor I, his cousin Fedor Romanov was regarded as the next in line of succession. Boris Godunov responded by incarcerating him in a monastery as the monk Filaret. Fedor's wife Xenia was forced to take the veil under the name of Martha, while their five-year-old son Michael was imprisoned along with his aunt Anastasia at the White Lake Monastery. When False Dmitry I captured the Russian throne, he promoted his "cousin"

The history of the Romanov dynasty begins with Fedor Nikitovich Romanov. In his youth, he was regarded as the finest rider and one of the most handsome men in Moscow. Appointed a boyar in 1586, Fedor held a series of important posts in the Russian government and army. He was related to Anastasia, the first wife of Ivan the Terrible.

Fedor to the rank of metropolitan of Rostov. Fedor Romanov preferred to side with the opposition, however, and played an active part in his overthrow. He was similarly unimpressed when False Dmitry II elected him patriarch of Russia. Fedor thought it better to politely decline such an offer, foreseeing the possible consequences of allying himself with a foreign usurper. He did, however, accept the post after helping to overthrow Basil Shuisky in May 1610. In April 1611, he headed an embassy to King Sigismund of Poland, who wanted to place his own son Wladyslaw on the Russian throne. During the negotiations, the patriarch was imprisoned and spent eight years in a Polish dungeon.

While Fedor Romanov was languishing in Poland, his son was elected tsar of Russia. The council convened to make the decision dispatched a large delegation of clergymen, boyars and public officials to Michael. The only problem was that no one in Moscow knew exactly where he was.

The delegates were commanded to "travel to His Majesty, Tsar and Grand Prince Michael Fedorovich of All the Russias, in Yaroslavl or wherever he might be." Armed with this order, the deputation set off to find their new sovereign. The Polish forces still occupying Russia also set out to find and kill the new tsar. They had more information than the

1617	Treaty of Stolbovo with Sweden.
1617–18	Prince Dmitry Pozharsky saves Moscow from a Polish invasion.
1630–32	Creation of the first foreign regiments, paving the way for a regular Russian army.
1634	Treaty of Polanów with Poland. Russia concedes several western territories and King Wladyslaw IV of Poland gives up his claim to the Russian throne.
1636	Fighting with the Crimean Tatars, who raid and plunder south Russia. The Belgorod Pale, an earthen rampart with fortresses, is built to protect Russia from Tatar incursions.
	Annexation of land in Siberia, discovery of the Pacific Ocean and establishment of diplomatic relations with China.
	Increased taxation of town dwellers to restore the country's financial situation.
	Presents of land to attract the nobility to state service. Increase in the bureaucratic apparatus.
	Establishment of a ten-year period to track down and capture runaway peasants.

Election of Michael Fedorovich Romanov (Muscovite Ambassadors Begging him to Accept the Crown in the Trinity Cathedral of the Ipatiev Monastery). Artist: Alexei Kivshenko

Alexei Tolstoy described the country inherited by Tsar Michael: "Three hundred years ago, the winds blew through the forests and steppe, across the enormous cemetery called Russia. Burnt city walls, towns and villages reduced to ashes, crosses and bones lining roads overgrown with grass, flocks of ravens and wolves howling in the night. The last bands of robbers stumbled along the forest paths, having long since drunk away ten years of pillage — boyars' furs, precious goblets and pearled icon settings. The country had been plundered and stripped bare."

Grand Apparel of Tsar Michael. 17th century.
Moscow Armoury

Eudokia Lukianovna
Streshneva

Russians on the whereabouts of Michael and his mother, whom they knew to be in the village of Domnino, fifty miles from Kostroma. Michael and his mother took refuge in the Ipatiev Monastery near Kostroma, where they were found by the delegates of the Land Council on 14 March 1613. When they asked Michael to accept the throne, his mother reminded the delegation that the Russian people had been disloyal to their rulers in times of trouble, saying that she would not let her son become tsar. After the envoys prayed, argued and finally threatened her, she conceded and gave her blessing. Michael then returned to Moscow with the delegation. Alexei Tolstoy described the country inherited by Tsar Michael: "Russia was ravaged and ruined. The Crimean Tatars stopped their incursions across the wild steppes, for there was nothing left to steal. For the past ten years, pretenders, thieves and Polish horsemen had passed this way with sabre and fire, from one end of Russia to the other. There was famine and plague; people ate horse manure and human salt-meat. Those who survived made their way north, towards the White Sea, the Urals and Siberia. On these difficult days, a boy was brought on a sledge across the dirty March roads to the charred walls of Moscow — a plundered and ravaged heap of ashes, only freed at great cost from the Polish occupants. A frightened boy elected tsar of Muscovy, at the advice of the patriarch, by impoverished boyars, empty-handed merchants and hard men from the north and the Volga. The boy prayed and wept, looking out of the window of his coach in fear and dejection at the ragged, frenzied crowds who had come to greet him at the gates of Moscow. The Russian people had little faith in the new tsar, but life had to go on..."

Michael Romanov was crowned tsar of Russia by Metropolitan Ephremus of Kazan on 11 July 1613. The tsar's uncle, Ivan Romanov, held the cap of Monomachus, Prince Trubetskoi bore the sceptre and Prince Pozharsky held the orb. During the coronation celebrations, the new sovereign rewarded those who had helped him to ascend the throne. Prince Pozharsky was made a boyar, while Kuzma Minin, a member of the duma council. Ivan Susanin's daughter Antonida and her husband Bogdan Sabinin were awarded half the village of Derevnische and all their descendants were freed from paying taxes. Michael Romanov was not particularly intelligent, strong or healthy. He was short-sighted and suffered from a weakness of the legs. He had a soft nature and was easily influenced by others. The new tsar was initially guided by his mother and her relatives, the Saltykov family, and then by his father, who returned from Poland in 1619. When Michael was twenty-eight, his mother sought a prospective bride for him and found Princess Maria Dolgorukova. Although Michael did not like his

Although one of the Polish detachments came close to Domnino, the village was in an inaccessible place and the Poles did not know how to get there. They ordered the head of the neighbouring village of Derevnische, Ivan Susanin, to take them to Domnino under pain of death. Pretending to take the Polish forces on a short cut, Susanin deliberately got them all lost in the forest. Although he was murdered by the angry Poles, Tsar Michael was saved. Ivan Susanin's heroic deed was immortalised in Mikhail Glinka's opera *A Life for the Tsar*.

Death of Ivan Susanin.
Artist: Alexei Markov

mother's choice, he dared not refuse her and the couple were married, but Maria fell ill during the wedding celebrations and died four months later. Michael's mother instantly began looking for a new bride. This time, her choice fell on Eudokia Streshneva. This union was more successful. Michael and Eudokia were married and had ten children.

Michael's reign witnessed several other events, perhaps not so important, yet nonetheless interesting. They include the public execution of Maryna Mniszech in Moscow, the construction of the Prison Yard in Moscow (1636), the capture by Cossacks of the Turkish fortress of Azov (1637) and the unsuccessful attempt to marry the tsar's eldest daughter, Irina, to Prince Valdemar of Denmark (1644).

In spring 1645, Tsar Michael contracted an illness of the stomach and kidneys and died at the age of forty-nine on the night of 12/13 June 1645. He was buried in the Archangel Cathedral.

Tsar Michael Sitting with Boyars in his State Room.
Artist: Andrei Ryabushkin

Tsar
Alexei Mikhailovich
1629–1676

Parents:

Tsar **Michael Fedorovich**
and Tsarina **Eudokia Lukianovna
Streshneva.**

Wives:

Maria Ilinichna Miloslavskaya
(1625–1669). Married: 16 January 1648.

Natalia Kirillovna Naryshkina
(1651–1694). Married: 22 January 1671.

Children of Alexis
and Maria Miloslavskaya:

Dmitry (1648–1649).

Eudokia (1650–1712). Although Eudokia
formally lived at the convent, she herself
never took the veil. Her personal icon —
Holy Virgin Mary Portaitissa Iviron
(Balkans, 17th century) — still hangs
in her former cell.

Martha (1652–1707). Baptised at the
Monastery of the Miracle. At the age of
forty-six, she was forced by Peter the
Great to enter the Covent of the Dormition in the Alexander Suburb for supporting his half-sister Sophie. Took the
veil as Sister Margaret.

Alexei (1654–1670).

Anna (1655–1659).

Sophia (see Sophie).

Ekaterina (1658–1718). St Catherine's
Hermitage was founded near the village
of Tsaritsyno in her honour. Her godparents were the future Empress Catherine I
and the Tsarevich Alexei Petrovich. Had
an extramarital affair with Yegor Yeli-
seyev, a priest from Kostroma.

Maria (1660–1723). Suspected of com-
plicity in a plot headed by Tsarevich
Alexei Petrovich, imprisoned at Schlüsselburg Fortress and placed under house
arrest in 1718. Released in 1721.
Buried in the Peter and Paul Fortress.

Fedor (see Fedor II).

Feodosia (1662–1713). Lived in St Petersburg from 1707. Buried alongside her
sister Martha at the Covent of the Dormition in the Alexander Suburb.

Simeon (1665–1669).

Ioann (see Ioann V).

Eudokia was born and died in Moscow
on 26–27 February 1669.

Children of Alexis and Natalia
Naryshkina:

Peter (see Peter I).

Natalia (1673–1716).

Feodora (1674–1677).

Alexis was the eldest son of Tsar Michael. He was born in Moscow on 9 March 1629 and baptised by Patriarch Filaret. Until the age of five, he was brought up by various wet-nurses. The boy's education was then entrusted to two boyars — Boris Morozov and Basil Streshnev. He also had a retinue of twenty stewards from distinguished Russian families.

Boris Morozov was influenced by Western ideas and Alexis developed an interest in European culture. The tsarevich was taught from primers and church books. He began writing at seven and, by the age of eleven, had his own small library of Russian and foreign literature, including grammar books, dictionaries and works on cosmography. His curriculum included music and the study of foreign maps and pictures. He grew up into a chubby, cheerful boy with red cheeks, a low forehead and twinkling eyes.

Alexis inherited the throne from his father at the age of sixteen and was crowned on 28 September 1645. The young tsar initially relied on the advice of others, particularly the cunning and ambitious Boris Morozov.

Alexis had a soft nature and a kind heart. Although he could be angry and strict, he was always fair, attempting to make peace with anyone who had aroused his wrath. He was deeply religious, observing all the Orthodox fasts and spending long hours in his private chapel. Although his subjects called him "Alexis the Most Meek", he was no coward, often accompanying the army into battle. He had a dignified poise and truly regal manners.

Alexis enjoyed reading and had a large library. He composed poems and prose and collected art. The tsar built a magnificent palace (unsurviving) at Kolomenskoe near Moscow. A landscape park, including ponds, greenhouses, gardens and the first Russian zoo, was laid out in Izmailovo, another estate outside Moscow. The first theatre in Russia was opened at Preobrazhenskoe, where religious plays, comedies and ballets were staged.

When the Time of Troubles was over and Tsar Michael Fyodorovich ascended the throne, there arose a necessity to renovate the royal residence demolished and burnt by the Poles. The temporary palace put up in 1614 was replaced in 1620 by another one constructed by the royal carpenter Isayev.

1646	Waves of public disorders, including the Salt Riots in Moscow.
1648	Establishment of an unlimited period to track down and capture runaway peasants. Annexation of Smolensk and Chernihiv. Abolition of the Land Council and the growing power of the autocracy.
1649	Compilation of a code of Russian laws.
1650	Annexation of western Ukraine (Pereyaslavl Rada).
1654–67	War with the Rzecz Pospolita or Polish-Lithuanian Commonwealth and the signing of the Treaty of Andrusovo (30 January 1667).
1656–58	War with Sweden and the signing of the Treaty of Roskilde (20 December 1658).
1658	Construction of new towns in Siberia — Nerchinsk, Irkutsk and Selenginsk.
1662	Copper Riot in Moscow.
1662–66	Foundation of regular infantry commanded by more than one hundred foreign officers.
1668–76	The Solovki Uprising.
1670–71	A revolt led by Stenka Razin.
	Construction of the first Russian naval vessels in the village of Dedilovo on the River Oka.

Moscow in the Mid-Seventeenth Century.
Artist: Apollinary Vasnetsov

In 1647, when he was eighteen, Alexis decided that the time had come to marry. He ordered two hundred of the most beautiful girls from leading Russian families to be assembled in Moscow. The tsar's choice fell on a maiden called Euphemia, the daughter of Fedor (Raf) Vsevolozhsky, a landlord from the Kasimov district.

Bedchamber in the Terem Palace
of the Moscow Kremlin

First Meeting of Tsar Alexis and Maria Miloslavskaya. Artist: Mikhail Nesterov

But as fires were frequent in Moscow, the building of a new stone palace was started by the masons Bazhen Ogurtsov, Lazar Ushakov, Trifon Sharutin, Antip Konstantinov and others. Its facades have come to us almost unaltered. The building looks very festive and picturesque thanks to its numerous pillars, cornices and entablature with tiled friezes as well as bands ornamented with polychrome tiles.

Besides literature, landscape gardening and the theatre, Alexis also enjoyed chess and hunting, particularly falconry. He kept over three thousand falcons and a hundred thousand

Alexis had a soft nature and a kind heart. Although he could be angry and strict, he was always fair, attempting to make peace with anyone who had aroused his wrath. He was deeply religious, observing all the Orthodox fasts and spending long hours in his private chapel. Although his subjects called him "Alexis the Most Meek", he was no coward, often accompanying the army into battle. He had a dignified poise and truly regal manners. Besides literature, landscape gardening and the theatre, Alexis also enjoyed chess and hunting.

Tsarina Embarking on a Pilgrimage during the Reign of Tsar Alexis.
Artist: Vyacheslav Schwartz

Maria Ilinichna
Miloslavskaya

Natalia Kirillovna
Naryshkina

pigeon-nests to provide them with fresh meat. The tsar did not only spend his time amusing himself, however. He coined the phrase "a time for work, an hour for play," which is now a national saying.

In 1647, Alexis decided that the time had come to marry. He ordered two hundred of the most beautiful girls from leading Russian families to be assembled in Moscow. The tsar's choice fell on a maiden called Euphemia, the daughter of Fedor (Raf) Vsevolozhsky, a landlord from the Kasimov district. As soon as Alexis's choice became known, rivals began plotting against Euphemia. Boris Morozov spread rumours that she suffered from fainting spells and was unable to bear children.

In the second half of the 17th century, the Terem palace became the main residence of Russian tsars. On the lower floor there were service areas and kitchens, and on the first floor articles of ceremonial attire were made in the Workshop Room. The second floor was occupied by the women's part, while the tsar's apartments took up the entire third floor. The palace interiors display a variety of fanciful ornaments and impress the visitor by their unusual planning.

Throne Room in the Terem Palace of the Moscow Kremlin

Palm Sunday in Moscow under Tsar Alexis. Procession of the Patriarch on a Donkey. Artist: Vyacheslav Schwartz

The Terem Palace interiors comprised the Dining Room, Golden Porch and Throne Room, Bedroom and Prayer Room. At the entrance to the Throne Room, or Tsar's Study, there is a pair of gilded statues of heraldic lions. As all the tsars wanted to emphasise the principle of royal succession, there are many representations of lions in the palace decor. A lion was a symbol of the ancient capital of Vladimir inherited by Moscow, the new capital of Russia. The colour of the walls decorated with the golden emblems of Russian principalities and cities used to be bright red, now it is crimson.

Patriarch Nikon and the Clergy.
Artist: Daniel Wuchters

The girl and her father were subsequently sent to Siberia for daring to conceal such important information from the tsar.

Boris Morozov immediately offered Alexis his own alternative — Maria Miloslavskaya, daughter of the steward Ilya Miloslavsky. The tsar agreed with his choice and married Maria. Maria's sister Anna married Boris Morozov, making the two men relatives. This factor helped to save Morozov from an unpleasant death in May 1648, when an angry mob invaded the Kremlin and demanded the execution of the hated boyars. Although the tsar gave the crowd two boyars — Plescheyev and Trakhanoiotov — he begged them to spare his brother-in-law, promising to remove him from all government posts. Boris was extremely unpopular in Moscow, where he was regarded as one of the main causes of national calamities. His house was ransacked during a second wave of disorders in 1662.

Golden (Red) Stairway of the Terem Palace
in the Moscow Kremlin

Tsar Alexis and Archbishop Nikon.
Artist: Alexander Litovchenko

Alexis's wife was extremely religious and they enjoyed a happy marriage. Maria bore him thirteen children before she died in 1669. Alexis was grief-stricken and made lavish gifts to the church in memory of her soul. After just over a year had passed, Alexis decided to remarry. He assembled seventy brides and selected the nineteen-year-old Natalia Naryshkina, the handsome daughter of a nobleman from Ryazan, Kirill Naryshkin. This beautiful young wife seemed to have a beneficial effect on the tsar, who began to look much younger. They lived together for five years and had three children.

Alexis backed the reform of the Russian Orthodox Church implemented by Patriarch Nikon in 1652. The original reason was the need to correct a number of errors that had crept into church books during the reign of Ivan the Terrible. Nikon decided to correct the mistakes by referring to the original Greek sources. As there were fundamental differences between the two churches, this led to important changes in the rites of the Russian Orthodox Church. Russians were now expected to cross themselves with three fingers, not two. Instead of bowing down to the ground, they were told to only genuflect as far as the waist.

Besides the mistakes in the church literature, Nikon also sought to correct many elements of Russian icon-painting. As all Russian icons depicted saints blessing with two fingers, many priests and members of the population regarded this as a direct attack on Orthodoxy. The Russian church divided into two irreconcilable groups — the supporters of Nikon and the Old Believers. Between 1654 and 1656,

One of the most outspoken opponents of Nikon's reforms was an archpriest called Avvakum. Avvakum was supported by Feodosia Morozova, the wife of a boyar called Morozov and a supporter of the old ways. Popularly known as "Boyarinya Morozova", she corresponded with Avvakum and gave financial assistance to his family. She was arrested in 1671 and incarcerated in the St Paphnutius of Borovsk Monastery, where she died in 1675.

Boyarinya Morozova.
Artist: Vasily Surikov

the opponents of Nikon's reforms were exiled or defrocked. In 1666, the church council officially condemned the Old Believers, calling on the civil authorities to burn to death anyone "daring to revile the Lord God."

One of the most outspoken opponents of Nikon's reforms was an archpriest called Avvakum. When he was asked to cross himself with three fingers, "his heart froze and his legs shook." Although Alexis personally sympathised with Avvakum, he was determined to overcome the Old Believers and banished the fiery priest to Tobolsk in 1653. Patriarch Nikon overreached himself, however, by openly encroaching upon the power of the tsar and he was defrocked in 1667.

After Nikon's dismissal, Avvakum was returned to Moscow by the enemies of the deposed patriarch. Yet Avvakum had no intention of reconciling himself to the reforms. He created special congregations of Old Believers, wrote

Torturing Boyarinya Morozova.
Unknown Artist

Stepan (Stenka) Razin (1630–1671) was a Don Cossack leader who led a major uprising against the Russian government. A colourful personality, he is the hero of many folk songs and legends. Razin's galleys raided the Persian coast of the Caspian Sea and occupied towns along the River Volga. When government forces eventually quelled the revolt, his commander fled to the River Don. Stepan Razin was betrayed by accomplices and brought to Moscow chained to a gallows, on an open scaffold. He was quartered alive on Red Square.

Stepan Razin.
Artist: Vasily Surikov

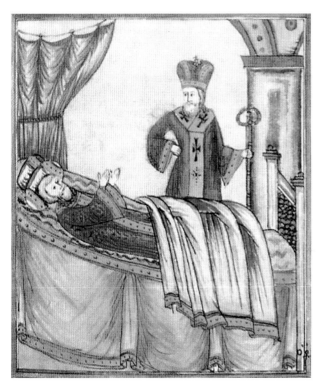

letters condemning Nikon's supporters and demanded that the tsar repeal the reforms. Alexis regarded his actions as tantamount to treason and he was exiled to Pustozersk in 1664. After a period of imprisonment in an "earth dungeon", he was burnt at the stake in 1681. Avvakum was supported by Feodosia Morozova, the wife of a boyar called Morozov and a supporter of the old ways. Boyarinya Morozova, she corresponded with Avvakum and gave financial assistance to his family. She was arrested in 1671 and died in 1675.

There was a whole host of less important events during the reign of Tsar Alexis. One was a decree requiring people to sign petitions to the tsar in the diminutive — "Ivashko" for Ivan or "Petrushko" for Peter. Another was the execution of the rebel Stenka Razin in Moscow in 1671.

Alexis once launched a campaign against swearing in Russia. He formed special detachments of Streltsy guards, who patrolled markets and other places where crowds gathered. Whenever they heard anyone swearing, they were ordered to beat the culprit with knouts and cudgels (themselves uttering even coarser oaths in the process).

Alexis died in Moscow on 29 January 1676 and was buried in the Archangel Cathedral.

Patriarch Nikon at the Bed of the Sick Tsar Alexis.
Miniature

Tsar
Fedor II
1661–1682

Parents:
Tsar **Alexei Mikhailovich** and
Tsarina **Maria Ilynichna Miloslavskaya.**

Wives:
Agatha Semenovna Grushetskaya,
the daughter of a waywode called
Semyon Grushetsky. Married: 1680.
Maria Matveevna Apraxina, daughter
of a notary called Matvei Vasilyevich
Apraxin. Married: 14 February 1681.

Fedor was born in Moscow on 30 May
1661 and crowned in the Dormition
Cathedral on 18 June 1676. Educated
by a monk called Simeon Polotsky, he
knew Polish and Latin and was interested in painting, literature and music. He helped to design the Lesser
Palace in the Moscow Kremlin, St Alexis's Church in the Monastery of the
Miracle and a palace in the village of
Vorobyovo.

To combat religious schismatics, Fedor planned to create an inquisition
based on the West European model,
but did not live to do so.

During his short reign, he nevertheless managed to do much good. He
banned the practice of burying wives
alive for the murder of their husbands;
the sentence was commuted to imprisonment in a nunnery. The mutila-
tion of thieves was also outlawed. The
boyars were no longer kept by the local population. Promotion to government posts depended on the tsar's personal opinion, rather than birth.
Handsome new buildings were built
of stone in the capital and other cities, including the Church of St John
the Baptist in Yarsolavl, the Rostov
Kremlin, the Krutitsy Monastery and
the Printing Works in Moscow. A handsome copy of the Gospels was created
in 1678, decorated with many draw-
ings and 1,200 miniatures.

Following the example of Kiev, a Slavonic, Greek and Latin Academy was
opened in Moscow, where young people could receive a Byzantine education. The first multiplication table was
printed in Russia.

Maria Matveevna
Apraxina. Lithograph

Fedor suffered from poor health after falling off a horse at the age of twelve. He was unable to put on his own hat and could only walk with the aid of a stick. Like his father, he suffered from scurvy and had a mild disposition, earning him the sobriquet "Fedor the Most Meek". Although the tsar disliked unnecessary ceremony, he was a stickler for order. He liked animals, opening a menagerie at Voskresenskoe and stud farms in other royal villages. The sickly young tsar was under the sway of Ivan Yazykov and Alexei Likhachev — two members of non-aristocratic families. In 1680, they married him to Agatha Grushetskaya, the daughter of a way-wode called Semyon Grushetsky. The following year, she died giving birth to a still-born son called Ilya. In the short time that they were married, Fedor was hopelessly dominated by Agatha, who supported the opening of Polish and Latin schools in Moscow and the shaving of beards. Less significant events include the reform of the court dress, replacing Russian caftans with Western clothes. The streets of Moscow were repaired and new houses were built of stone.

The tsar remarried on 14 February 1682. This time, his choice fell on one of Ivan Yazykov's relatives — the seventeen-year-old Maria Apraxina, daughter of a notary called Matvei Apraxin.

Fedor II died in Moscow on 27 April 1682, two months after he married his second wife and one month before his twenty-first birthday. He was buried in the Archangel Cathedral. The tsar did not leave any surviving issue.

1677	Founding of the Slavonic, Greek and Latin Academy in Moscow.
1678	General census of the population.
1679	Abolition of the practice of mutilation.
1681	Signing of peace treaties with Turkey and the Crimea (1681). Turkey recognises Kiev as a Russian town and is awarded the Trans-Dnieper region.
1682	The boyars were no longer kept by the local population. Promotion to government posts depended on the tsar's personal opinion, rather than birth.

Less significant events include the reform of the court dress, replacing Russian caftans with Western clothes.

The streets of Moscow were repaired and new houses were built of stone.

Tug. Second half of the 17th century. Moscow Armoury
Augsburg. Master J. Minlich

Princesses' Terem.
Artist: Baron Mikhail von Klodt

Regent
Sophie
1657–1704

Parents:
Tsar **Alexei Mikhailovich** and
Tsarina **Maria Ilynichna Miloslavskaya.**

Sophie was born in Moscow on 17 September 1657. She received an excellent education from Simeon Polotsky, learning both Latin and Polish. She studied history and wrote poems and plays. Although physically unattractive, she more than made up for this with her quick mind, energy and ambition.

After the death of Fedor II in 1682, the Streltsy guards supported Sophie's demand to be made co-ruler alongside the two young tsars — ten-year-old Peter

Prince Vasily Vasilyevich Golitsyn.
Lithograph

and sixteen-year-old Ioann. On 29 May 1682, she was formally proclaimed the regent. Sophie ruled with the help of her lover, the intelligent and handsome Prince Vasily Golitsyn. She sent Peter and his mother to live in the village of Preobrazhenskoe, while the sickly Ioann was no match for his elder sister and Prince Golitsyn, who quickly concentrated power in their own hands.

Sophie's image was struck on Russian coins from 1684 onwards and she assumed the title of autocrat in 1686. Fearing only the schismatics and the guards, she persecuted the Old Believers and destroyed the power of the Streltsy.

Sophie's dream of ruling Russia on her own was thwarted by Peter the Great,

Sophie was accused of treason and banished to the Novodevichy Convent. She spent the rest of her life as a nun, guarded by one hundred men. Before she died, she took the *schema* — the highest and strictest monastic discipline.

Streltsy Rebellion.
Artist: Nikolai Dmitriyev-Orenburgsky

who pursued his own independent line after marrying in January 1689. His half-sister attempted to dethrone him with the help of the Streltsy guards in August 1689, but Peter was supported by his own forces. Many boyars and public officials refused to side with the ambitious regent against the lawful tsar. She was accused of treason and banished to the Novodevichy Convent. In 1698, when Peter was abroad, Sophie attempted to seize power again with the help of the Streltsy guards. The rebellion was quickly defeated and she was forced to become a nun. Peter executed a total of 1,182 Streltsy guards, several of whom were left hanging outside Sophie's prison cell at the convent. Sophie spent the rest of her life as a nun, guarded by one hundred men. Before she died, she took the *schema* — the highest and strictest monastic discipline. She died on 3 July 1704 and was buried in the Smolensk Cathedral of the Novodevichy Convent.

Arrest of Tsarevna Sophie.
Artist: Ilya Repin

One of the less important events under Sophie was a public debate between the church authorities and the Old Believers in the Palace of Facets on 5 July 1682. The event was attended by Patriarch Joachim, archbishops and several members of the royal family, including Sophie's sisters, Alexis's sister Tatyana and his second wife Natalia Naryshkina. Archbishop Athanasius of Kholmogory spoke on behalf of the authorities, while Nikita Pustosvyat represented the schismatics. During the debate, Nikita Pustosvyat fell on the archbishop, knocking him off his feet — to the delight of the Streltsy guards, who were mostly Old Believers. Sophie later executed Nikita Pustosvyat and burnt many schismatics at the stake.

1685	Last tributes paid to the khan of Crimea.
1686	Conclusion of "eternal peace" with Poland, recognising Russia's right to Smolensk, Kiev and western Ukraine.
1687	Opening of the Slavonic, Greek and Latin Academy in Moscow.
1689	Signing of the Treaty of Nerchinsk with China, establishing the Sino-Russian border.

Tsarevna Sophie at the Novodevichy Convent during the Execution of the Streltsy Guards. Artist: Ilya Repin

Tsar
Ioann V
1666–1696

Parents:

Tsar **Alexei Mikhailovich**
and Tsarina **Maria Miloslavskaya.**

Wife:

Praskovia Fedorovna Saltykova
(1664–1723). Married: January 1684.

Children of Ioann V and Praskovia:

Maria (1689–1692). Her godparents were Peter I and his aunt Tatyana.

Feodosia (1690–1691). Her godparents were Peter I and his aunt Tatyana.

Ekaterina (1691–1733). Her godparents were Peter I and his aunt Tatyana. She was a lively girl who adored dancing. Chubby and talkative, she won many admirers at balls in St Petersburg with her merry disposition and humorous nature. In 1717, Peter the Great gave her in marriage to Duke Carl Leopold of Mecklenburg-Schwerin. The following year, she gave birth to the future Regent Anna Leopoldovna. She did not get on with her brutal and despotic husband and left him in 1722 (he was later overthrown and died in prison). Ekaterina was delighted to return to Russia, where she threw herself into a life of balls and banquets. She put on so much weight that Peter the Great ordered her to control her appetite, without success. On 14 June 1733, she died of dropsy at the age of forty-two.

Anna (see Empress Anna Ioannovna).

Praskovia (1694–1731). Unlike her elder sisters, she was blessed with good looks and soon demonstrated a streak of independence. Although Peter the Great hoped to marry her to a European prince, she fell in love with Ivan Dmitriyev-Mamonov, an elderly general descended from Prince Rurik. She insisted on marrying him and Peter eventually agreed. After marrying in 1723, they lived at Praskovia's estate on the River Moika in St Petersburg, which they later presented to the Semyonovsky Life Guards Regiment (Ivan was an officer in the regiment, which did not have any headquarters in the new capital). They moved to Izmailovo, where Praskovia staged performances at her domestic theatre. Ivan suddenly died in May 1730, while their only son died at the age of five.

Ioann V was born in Moscow on 27 August 1666. All his life, he had poor health. He suffered from scurvy, dizzy attacks, poor sight and a speech impediment. When Fedor II died, Patriarch

On 26 May 1682, the duma of boyars announced that Ioann would be the elder and Peter the junior tsar, with Sophie as regent. The two boys were crowned at the Dormition Cathedral on 25 June 1682. A second cap of Monomachus was specially made for Peter, who sat alongside his half-brother on a double throne, with a separate bench for Sophie.

Tsars Ioann Alexeyevich and Peter Alexeyevich. Engraving

Joachim and the boyars decided that the throne should pass to Peter and led the courtiers, civil servants, army and the people of Moscow in swearing an oath to the ten-year-old boy. The Miloslavsky clan, however, began to spread rumours that the Naryshkin family had murdered Peter's brother, Ioann. Rioting broke out in Moscow on 23 May 1682, during which the Streltsy guards killed several relatives and friends of Natalia Naryshkina, including Artamon Matveyev and Prince Dolgorukov. In an attempt to quell the rebellion, Ioann was shown to the guards, who demanded that he too be crowned tsar. A council of the upper clergy and government met in urgent session and decided that there would be two tsars. When Ioann reached seventeen, Sophie chose a bride for him. This was Praskovia Saltykova, who was related to the Romanovs and other aristocratic families. Tall and beautiful, she was the daughter of the steward and waywode Fedor Saltykov. When she learnt of Sophie's plans, the lovely Praskovia was horrified, declaring that she would die rather than marry the weak and sickly Ioann. Sophie was not interested in her opinion, however, and the couple were married in January 1684. Between them, they had five daughters. Ioann was paralysed at the age of twenty-seven and died two years later, on 29 January 1696. He was buried in the Archangel Cathedral. Praskovia survived her husband by twenty-seven years. As the years passed, she lost her former good looks. She grew flabby, suffered from dropsy and was confined to a wheelchair. She died in St Petersburg in 1723.

After Peter managed to remove Sophie from power in 1689, Ioann continued to be regarded as co-tsar. Although they signed all official documents together, Ioann played little role in the running of the state, spending his time "in constant prayer and fasting." He was, in the words of historian Vasily Klyuchevsky, "a mere figurehead, brought out on special occasions." He nevertheless managed to maintain good relations with both Sophie and Peter.

Double Throne of Tsars Ioann Alexeyevich and Peter Alexeyevich. 1682–84. Moscow Armoury

Coronation of Tsars Ioann V and Peter I on 25 June 1682

Emperor
Peter I
1672–1725

Parents:

Tsar **Alexei Mikhailovich** and
Tsarina **Natalia Kirillovna Naryshkina.**

Wives:

Eudokia Fedorovna (Praskovia Illarionovna) Lopukhina, the daughter Illarion Abramovich Lopukhin (1670–1731). Married: 27 January 1689.

Catherine I Alexeyevna (1684–1727), the daughter of Samuel Skowronski. Married: 19 February 1712.

Children of Peter I and Eudokia:

Alexei (1690–1718). He grew up at Pre-obrazhenskoe under the watchful eye of Tsarevna Natalia Alexeyevna. He learnt French, German and basic arithmetic, but had a poor knowledge of geometry and military tactics. In 1709, he was sent to study in Dresden, where he acquired a taste for reading, assembling a large library. In 1710, Peter the Great decided that Alexei should marry Princess Charlotte Christina Sophie of Brunswick-Wolfenbüttel. They were married in Torgau on 14 December 1711. Despite their dislike for one another, they managed to have two children — Natalia in 1714 and the future Peter II in 1715. After giving birth to Peter, Charlotte contracted post-natal fever and died. She was so unhappy with her husband that she refused all medicines and deliberately ate things that could only do her harm. Sixteen days after the birth of Alexei's son Peter, his father's second wife, Catherine I, gave birth to a son, also called Peter. Catherine and Prince Menshikov did not like Alexei and began a deliberately campaign of defamation. Peter the Great told his son to either help him rule Russia or become a monk. Alexei preferred the latter option. When his father went to Denmark in 1716, he fled to Austria, taking refuge with his former brother-in-law, Emperor Charles VI. When Peter the Great learnt of his son's flight, he sent Peter Tolstoy to find him. Tolstoy tracked him down and returned Alexei to Moscow. A plot against Peter the Great was uncovered and the ringleaders were executed. Peter appointed a supreme court of generals, senators, senior clergymen and guards officers, who sentenced Alexei to death. On 26 June 1718, he died in unclear circumstances in the Trubetskoi bastion of the Peter and Paul Fortress and was buried in the St Peter and St Paul Cathedral.

Alexander (1691–1692).

Pavel was born and died in 1693.

Peter I on the Toy (*Poteshny*) Manoeuvres.
Artist: Alexei Kivshenko

Peter I and Lefort (Manoeuvres of the Toy Fleet
on Lake Plescheyevo). Artist: Dmitry Kardovsky

The subject of countless books, films and works of art, Peter the Great is probably the most famous member of the Romanov family. He single-handedly changed the course of Russian history, turning the country into a powerful empire ranking alongside the other European powers. The imperial period of Russian history begins with Peter I.

Peter was born in Moscow on 30 May 1672 and baptised at the Monastery of the Miracle on 29 June 1672. He began walking at the age of six months. At the age of five, he was introduced to his first tutor — Nikita Zotov, a deacon of the petitions department. Although he learnt to read and write, he did not receive a good education.

On the death of his father on 27 April 1682, Peter was proclaimed tsar at the age of ten. The intrigues of the

1696	Creation of the Russian high seas fleet. Young noblemen sent abroad to study. Foundation of a system of orders.
1699	Opening of the Academy of Gunners.
1700	Adoption of the Julian calendar, counting the new year from 1 January and not 1 September and the year from the birth of Christ and not the creation of the world.
	Formation of guards regiments.
	Signing of the Treaty of Constantinople with Turkey.
1701	Opening of a School of Mathematical and Navigational Sciences in Moscow.
1703	Foundation of St Petersburg, later the capital of Russia (1712). Foundation of the first Russian newspaper *Vedomosti*.
1705	Introduction of conscription.
1708–09	Formation of eight (later ten) provinces headed by governors to replace the old system of districts, waywodeships and governorships. The provinces are later divided into forty-seven regions (1719).
1708–10	Introduction of the Russian "civil" alphabet.
1710–11	End of the Russo-Turkish War.
1711	Replacement of the duma of boyars with the Senate.
1714	Decree of primogeniture transferring property to one son and strengthening the nobility's hold on the land.
1715	Opening of a Naval Academy in St Petersburg.
1716	Introduction of the Military Code.
1718	Replacement of the offices with colleges.
1719	Opening of a School of Engineering and Artillery in St Petersburg.
	Opening of the first museum (Kunstkammer) and public library in St Petersburg.
1720	Introduction of the Naval Code.
1721	Signing of the Treaty of Nystad with Sweden, giving Russia territory along the River Neva, Karelia, the Baltic provinces and the towns of Narva, Revel, Riga and Vyborg. Russia becomes an empire with the tsar as emperor. Replacement of the patriarchate with the Holy Synod.
1722	Formation of the table of ranks — promotion in the army, navy and civil service is now based on personal abilities, rather than descent.
1722–23	Russo-Persian War giving Russia the western shores of the Caspian Sea and the towns of Derbent and Baku.
1723	The peasantry becomes the personal property of the nobility.
1724	Foundation and opening of the Academy of Sciences, with a grammar school and university in St Petersburg.

In 1697, Peter the Great decided to go on a fact-finding mission to Europe. The Great Embassy left Moscow in March, with the tsar travelling incognito as "Peter Mikhailov, sergeant of the Preobrazhensky Regiment." Peter I visited Holland, England, Germany and Austria, where he studied shipbuilding, anatomy, dentistry and many other skills and crafts.

Portrait of Peter I.
Artist: Gottfried Kneller

Peter I Studying the Theory
of Shipbuilding. Unknown Artist

Peter I Making a Rudder.
Artist: Baron Mikhail von Klodt

Peter I Studying Shipbuilding
in Zaandam.
Artist: Claudius Lebedev

Prince Fedor Romodanovsky of the Preobrazhensky Office launched an official investigation into the Streltsy revolt. Streltsy guards were executed *en masse*, with Peter himself chopping off several heads. In February 1699, the Streltsy detachments were disbanded and any surviving guards were banished to the far reaches of the country.

Morning of the Streltsy Sentence.
Artist: Vasily Surikov

Miloslavsky family, however, led to the Streltsy revolt and the murder of his mother's allies in Moscow in May 1682. The upshot was the crowning of two co-tsars with Sophie as regent. Peter and his mother were forced to leave Moscow and live in Preobrazhenskoe, once the favourite place of their father. Preobrazhenskoe became a temporary royal residence or, in the words of Vasily Klyuchevsky, "a stopping place on the way to St Petersburg."

Peter was haunted by the memories of the Streltsy uprising and fears for the future. There was no force at Preobrazhenskoe capable of defending him and his mother should the Streltsy revolt break out again. He decided to set about creating his own army. Besides the children of boyars, the tsar was joined at Preobrazhenskoe by a large number of courtiers. From their

Peter I Catching Plotters in the House of Ziekler. Artist: Adolph Charlemágne

In 1695 and 1696, Peter the Great led two attempts to capture the Turkish fortress of Azov. The second attempt was successful and Peter founded a Russian fleet at Azov. On 20 October 1696, at Peter's command, the duma of boyars announced the creation of a high seas fleet. Russia was not only to be a great continental power, but also a great naval power. Construction of a regular Russian navy began on 4 November 1696.

Taking of Azov on 18 July 1696.
Artist: Sir Robert Kerr Porter

Francis Lefort — First Russian Admiral and Participant of the Azov Campaigns
Portrait of Alexander Menshikov.
Unknown Artist

ranks he formed a toy (*poteshny*) brigade, which gradually, under the guise of childhood games, turned into a military unit. This detachment was called the Preobrazhensky Toy Regiment. When the number of amateur forces grew, a second battalion was formed in the neighbouring village of Semyonovskoe, called the Semyonovsky Toy Regiment. The forces were trained by foreign officers in the West European manner. They fought mock battles with real weapons, often leading to serious injuries and several deaths. Peter's steward, Prince Ivan Dolgoruky, was killed during one such battle, while the tsar's face was badly burnt in an artillery barrage. The first mock battles were more like village fistfights. The two regiments would line up against a detachment of Streltsy guards on the bank of the River Yauza. Brawny representatives of each "army" came forward and began insulting one another. The situation became increasingly heated, with the two sides eventually coming to blows. The foreign instructors gradually began to develop these battles into regular manoeuvres along Western lines. A fortress called Pressburg — a miniature copy of the fort in modern-day Bratislava — was built on the River Yauza to study the art of defending and besieging fortifications. Besides infantry formations, there were also artillery and cavalry detachments and a toy navy on Lake Pereyaslavl.

Peter the Great developed Russian industry, opening many new factories, mills and mines and building the Vyshny Volochek and Ladoga Canals. The merchant class was divided into guilds, while craftsmen were grouped in corporations. Medical institutes, a public theatre and schools of translators were opened. New forms of clothing, assemblies, taxes and letterhead notepaper were introduced. New silver coins were minted. The reforms of Peter the Great affected virtually every aspect of Russian life.

Peter I Steering a Sailing Boat.
Table silver decoration

The toy forces were officially renamed the Preobrazhensky and Semyonovsky regiments in 1687. The four hundred officers were mostly foreigners, although only Russian noblemen could be the sergeants. Both regiments were headed by General Artamon Golovin. The size of the regiments gradually grew. By the mid-1690s, the Preobrazhensky Regiment counted ten companies, including a bomber squad. The Preobrazhensky and Semyonovsky regiments gave Peter the means to defend himself from potential enemies and a tool to resolve important matters of state. In August 1689, he learnt that Sophie and her new lover, Fedor Shaklovity, were preparing a *coup d'etat*. Peter left Preobrazhenskoe for the safety of the Trinity Monastery at Sergiev Posad, where he was joined by the Preobrazhensky and Semyonovsky regiments. He managed to iso-

Mock Naval Battle on the IJ in Honour of Tsar Peter I in September 1697.
Detail. Artist: A. Abraham

late and overthrow the "third, discreditable person," as he referred to Sophie in his letters to his brother Ioann. She was incarcerated in the Novodevichy Convent, while her Streltsy supporters went to the scaffold.

Peter did not abandon his war games after securing his hold on the throne. He entrusted all affairs of state to his mother, a shrewd, but, however, not very intelligent woman. She was helped

On 16 May 1703, Peter the Great laid the foundations of a fort on Zayachy (Hare) Island, not far from the mouth of the River Neva. The construction was based on the tsar's own design and became known as the Peter and Paul Fortress. On the surrounding marshlands, Peter planned to build a new town and port. The city was originally named *Piterburkh* or the "town of St Peter." St Petersburg was the capital of Russia from the 1710s to 1918.

Peter the Great. Foundation of St Petersburg.
Artist: Alexei Venetsianov

St Petersburg. View onto the Summer
Palace of Peter I in the Summer Gardens

Panorama of the Peter and Paul Fortress
in St Petersburg

Peter the Great had an iron will and boundless energy. He was ambitious, intuitive, despotic, courageous, cruel and self-assured. The tsar could be decisive, forceful, convulsive and fidgety. He combined an amazing capacity for work with an equally unquenchable thirst for amusement.

by Prince Vasily Golitsyn (a heavy drinker and a shrewd politician) and her brother Lev (a heavy drinker and a poor politician). Her council included Tikhon Streshnev, a master of intrigue whom many believed to be Peter's real father. The tsar often referred to him as "father" and appointed him minister of war in 1701. In his poem *Russia*, Maximilian Voloshin describes one of Peter's attempts to learn the truth of his origin:

> The tsar, in his cups, interrogated
> Streshnev on the rack:
> "Tell me, am I your son or not?"
> "The devil knows who you are;
> The tsarina was often on her back!"

Natalia Naryshkina took sometimes independent decisions, such as the decree banishing the Jesuits from Russia or the burning of Kulman the Mystic at the stake on Red Square. Patrick Gordon, a Scottish general in Russian service, complained in a letter to London in July 1690 that Peter was completely uninterested in governing. He divided his time between drinking sessions and toy battles, leading what Vasily Klyuchevsky called "the life of a homeless, itinerant student." The Crimean Tatars, meanwhile, defeated Prince Golitsyn and captured a number of Russian provinces. Russia's prestige in Europe fell. When a new sultan assumed power in Turkey, he informed all the European rulers, with the exception of the Russian tsar. When Peter's mother died in 1694, he was forced to take over the running of the state. In 1695 and 1696, he

Cabin of Peter I on Petrovskaya Embankment
in St Petersburg

Peter I.
Artist: Valentin Serov. Detail

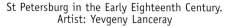

Petersburg became the primary concern and favourite "child of the northern giant, in which the energy, brutality and revolutionary force of the '93 Convention were concentrated … *the favourite child* of the tsar, who renounced his country for its own good and oppressed it in the name of Europeanism and civilisation" (Alexander Herzen).

St Petersburg in the Early Eighteenth Century.
Artist: Yevgeny Lanceray

travelling incognito as "Peter Mikhailov, sergeant of the Preobrazhensky Regiment." Peter I visited Holland, England, Germany and Austria, where he studied shipbuilding, anatomy, dentistry and many other skills and crafts. His plans to visit Italy in 1698 were thwarted when he received news of another revolt of the Streltsy guards in support of Sophie. Although the tsar hurried back to Moscow, by the time he arrived the revolt had already been put down by his toy regiments.

led two attempts to capture the Turkish fortress of Azov. The second attempt was successful and Peter founded a Russian fleet at Azov. In 1697, he decided to go on a fact-finding mission to Europe. The Great Embassy left Moscow in March, with the tsar

Peter I in Mon Plaisir at Peterhof
Artist: Valentin Serov

Prince Fedor Romodanovsky of the Preobrazhensky Office launched an official investigation into the revolt. Streltsy guards were executed *en masse*, with Peter himself chopping off several heads. In February 1699, the Streltsy detachments were disbanded and any surviving guards were banished to the far reaches of the country.

Peter decided to make a clean sweep by confining his wife Eudokia to a convent. When he was nineteen, his mother had married him to the sixteen-year-old daughter of Illarion Lopukhin on 27 January 1689. Although her name was actually Praskovia Illarionovna, Peter's mother thought that Eudokia sounded better. She did not like the father's name either and he was forced to change it to Fedor. Praskovia Illarionovna thus became Eudokia Fedorovna. Prince Boris Kurakin describes her as a handsome girl of "only average intelligence." Peter and Eudokia's marriage was initially happy. Eudokia gave birth to a son called Alexei in 1690, followed by two more boys. Peter then tired of his wife and began a relationship with Anna Mons, the daughter of a wine trader in the German Suburb (foreigners' settlement).

Following the breakdown of their marriage, Peter decided to rid himself of Eudokia. He banished her to the Convent of the Intercession in Suzdal on 23 September 1698. The following year, he sent Semyon Yazykov to the convent to inform Eudokia that she was to join the sisterhood as Sister Helen. In 1709, Peter's former wife began a nine-year

Perspective up the River Neva from the Admiralty and Academy of Sciences to the East. Engraving by Mikhail Makhayev

In April 1709, the Swedish army besieged the strategic Ukrainian town of Poltava. Peter rushed south with Russian forces and a battle was fought on 27 June 1709. The Russian army scored a brilliant victory, which was also of great political importance. Sweden never recovered from the blow.

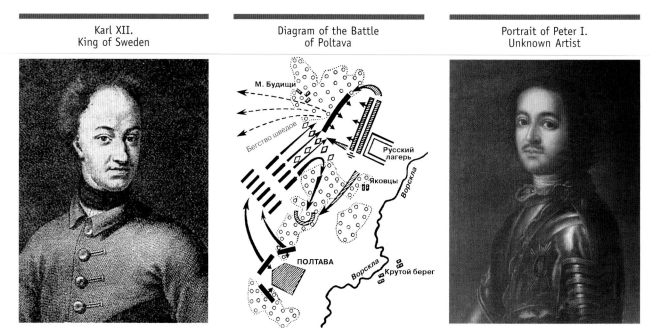

Karl XII.
King of Sweden

Diagram of the Battle
of Poltava

Portrait of Peter I.
Unknown Artist

love affair with Captain Stepan Glebov. This came to light in 1718, when the tsar was investigating the flight abroad of their son, Tsarevich Alexei. Both were harshly punished. Stepan Glebov was impaled, while Eudokia was tortured and moved to the Convent of the Dormition in Staraya (Old) Ladoga.

Eudokia's troubles did not end there. When Peter's second wife ascended the throne in 1725, she was imprisoned at Schlüsselburg and only released in October 1727, during the reign of her grandson, Peter II. The former tsarina spent the rest of her life at the Novodevichy Convent in Moscow, where she died in 1731. She was buried there alongside three of Peter's half-sisters — Sophie, Ekaterina and Eudokia.

Much has been written about Peter's physical appearance, particularly his great height. The closest physical likeness to the tsar is Mikhail Shemyakin's famous statue in the Peter and Paul Fortress. Valentin Serov, a *fin-de-siècle* Russian artist who painted a series of works dedicated to Peter the Great, a figure he admired, compiled his own image of the tsar: "It is regretful that a man who did not have a single jot of sweetness about him is always portrayed as some operatic hero or beauty. He was frightening to look at — a long body on thin, scrawny legs, with such a small head in comparison to the

Battle of Poltava.
Artist: Alexander Kotzebue

Alexei was forced to renounce his rights to the throne in favour of his half-brother Peter and to inform on those who had helped him to flee to Austria. The investigation continued when the court moved to St Petersburg in March 1718. A plot against Peter the Great was uncovered and the ring-leaders were executed. Peter appointed a supreme court of generals, senators, senior clergymen and guards officers, who sentenced Alexei to death.

rest of the body that he must have looked more like a scarecrow with a badly fitting head than a living person. He was forever grimacing, winking, twitching his mouth and slapping his chin. He took enormous strides and his companions were forced to run to keep up with him. I can imagine what a monster he must have seemed to foreigners and how frightening he was to the people of St Petersburg. A freak with a constantly twitching head ... a terrible person."

Peter had a nervous character. He was quick to fly into a rage, when his face would begin to twitch — possibly a nervous reaction brought on by the shock of the Streltsy revolt in his childhood. Vasily Klyuchevsky noted another of his traits: "In keeping with Old Russian habits, Peter did not like wide rooms or high ceilings. He always avoided magnificent royal palaces whenever he was abroad. A son of the endless Russian steppe, he felt suffocated among the hills of a narrow German valley. Strangely enough, growing up in the open air and accustomed to wide spaces, he could not live in a room with a high ceiling. Whenever he found himself in one, he would order a special canvas ceiling to be hung low. Perhaps the cramped conditions of his childhood had left its mark on him."

Peter I Interrogating Tsarevich Alexei at Peterhof.
Artist: Nikolai Ge

Peter the Great had an iron will and boundless energy. He was ambitious, intuitive, despotic, courageous, cruel and self-assured. The tsar could be decisive, forceful, convulsive and fidgety. He combined an amazing capacity for work with an equally unquenchable thirst for amusement. His curious and lively mind led him to acquire knowledge in many different crafts and sciences, including shipbuilding, artillery, fortifications, diplomacy, military tactics, mechanics, medicine and astronomy. The tsar held audiences with such leading scientists

Tsarina Eudokia Fedorovna, First Wife of Peter I, in Nun's Habit. Drawing

Tsarevich
Alexei Petrovich

Princess Charlotte,
Wife of Tsarevich Alexei Petrovich

In autumn 1718, Peter announced his intention of introducing a new concept into the life of St Petersburg — informal gatherings or forums called assemblies: "Assembly comes from the French word *assemblée* and cannot be translated into one word in Russian. A meeting in a house, not only for entertainment, but also for business. A place where people can meet, talk and hear what is being done and where it is being done, accompanied by entertainment."

Assembly at the Court of Peter I.
Artist: Claudius Lebedev

Peter I Walking in the Summer Gardens.
Artist: Alexander Benois

as Gottfried Wilhelm Leibnitz and Sir Isaac Newton and was elected an honorary member of the French Academy of Sciences in 1717.

Peter the Great developed Russian industry, opening many new factories, mills and mines and building the Vyshny Volochek and Ladoga Canals. The merchant class was divided into guilds, while craftsmen were grouped in corporations. Medical institutes, a public theatre and schools of translators were opened. New forms of clothing, assemblies, taxes and letterhead notepaper were introduced. New silver coins were minted. The reforms of Peter the Great affected virtually every aspect of Russian life. Peter created a pyramidal form of state structure. The peasantry served the nobility, the nobility served the monarch and the monarch served the state.

On 5 February 1722, Peter signed a decree altering the way in which the Russian throne was inherited. Instead of the crown passing from father to son, the sovereign would henceforth nominate his own successor from the members of his family. In 1724, Peter signed a document bequeathing the throne to Catherine, who was crowned empress in the Dormition Cathedral in Moscow on 7 May 1724. Later that year, Peter learnt of Catherine's love affair with the chamberlain William Mons. They were only discovered by accident, during an investigation into an accusation of bribery and embezzlement. William Mons was executed and Peter tore up the document naming Catherine as his successor.

Peter began 1725 in poor health. On 16 January, he took to his bed. The pains grew worse and his groans and cries could be heard throughout the palace. Under the terms of his manifesto changing the rules of inheritance, the emperor was obliged to name his own successor. On 27 January, he sat down to write his will, but only managed to command *Leave everything to...*

On 28 January 1725, Peter died in great pain from a stone in his bladder.

In 1724, on a cold and stormy night in October, Peter the Great was sailing from Kronstadt to St Petersburg when he heard cries for help from the sea, not far from the village of Lakhta. A warship had struck a sandbank and was sinking. The tsar immediately set off in their direction. Standing up to his waist in icy water, he helped to save the sailors, aggravating the disease that eventually killed him.

State Room in the Mon Plaisir Palace
at Peterhof

He was buried in the still unfinished St Peter and St Paul Cathedral in St Petersburg. The tsar was officially proclaimed "Emperor Peter the Great of All the Russias." Many, however, believed that he was the Antichrist, sent to punish Russia for her sins. Public opinion was sharply split over the merits of his reign.

Peter the Great died without leaving an official heir. A meeting of senators, clergymen, generals and guards officers was split over who should inherit the throne. Members of the old aristocracy — the Dolgoruky, Golitsyn and Repnin families — wanted to offer the crown to Alexei's son Peter, the eleven-year-old grandson of Peter the Great. They regarded Catherine as a Lithuanian laundress not worthy of even approaching the Russian throne. Peter's protégés — Menshikov, Yaguzhinsky and Tolstoy — supported Catherine. The second group carried the day thanks to the brilliant oratory of Archbishop Feofan Prokopovich and the actions of General Ivan Buturlin, who stationed two guards regiments beneath the palace windows. Catherine was declared empress, and captain of the Bomber Squad.

Peter the Great Saving Drowning Sailors at Lakhta.
Artist: Pyotr Shamshin

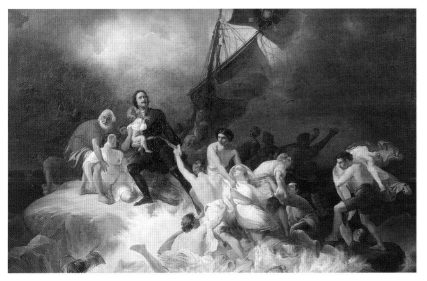

Peter I on his Death Bed.
Artist: Ivan Nikitin

Empress Catherine I
1684–1727

Father: Lithuanian peasant called
Samuel Skowronski (from the Polish word for lark — *skowronek*).

Husband:
Emperor **Peter I Alexeyevich.**

Children of Peter I and Catherine I:

Peter (1704–1707).

Pavel (1705–1707).

Ekaterina (1706–1708).

Anna (1708–1728). She was an intelligent girl who read widely and learnt four foreign languages — French, German, Italian and Swedish. Contemporaries described her as a "brunette as pretty as an angel." In 1720, Duke Carl Friedrich of Holstein-Gottorp came to St Petersburg to marry a Russian princess. On 23 November 1724, Carl Friedrich signed a marriage contract, agreeing to give up any claims to the Russian throne on behalf of himself, Anna and their children. A secret clause, however, stated that Peter could take any son of their marriage to Russia and make him the heir to the throne. The couple were married at the Trinity Cathedral in St Petersburg on 21 May 1725. Carl Friedrich and Anna spent the next two years in St Petersburg. Catherine I made her son-in-law a member of the privy council. He began to play an important role in the life of the Russian Empire and foreign diplomats predicted that the empress would make Anna her successor. When Catherine died in 1727, Alexander Menshikov forced them to leave Russia. Anna gave birth to a son — Carl Peter Friedrich (the future Peter III) — on 10 February 1728. She died three months later. Her body was brought back to St Petersburg and buried in the St Peter and St Paul Cathedral.

Elizaveta (see Elizabeth Petrovna).

Natalia (1713–1715).

Margarita (1714–1715).

Peter (1715–1719). Favourite child of Peter and Catherine. Declared the heir to the Russian throne in 1718. Died of an incurable disease in St Petersburg.

Pavel was born in Wesel in Westphalia on 2 January 1717. Died the following day.

Natalia (1718–1725). Died of measles in St Petersburg and buried on the same day as her father.

Peter (1719–1723). Peter the Great was extremely upset at his death, which removed the last chance to see a son on the Russian throne.

Order
of St Catherine

Catherine I was the daughter of a Lithuanian peasant called Samuel Skowronski (from the Polish word for lark — *skowronek*). She was born in Livonia on 5 April 1684 and baptised into the Roman Catholic Church under the name of Martha. Orphaned at the age of twelve, she was taken into the service of a pastor from Roop and converted to Lutheranism. She then went to work for a minister called Gluck in Marienburg, where she studied housekeeping, handicrafts and the Protestant religion. In 1702, when Martha was eighteen, she received an offer of marriage from a Swedish dragoon called Johann. This was in the middle of the Great Northern War between Russia and Sweden for an outlet to the Baltic Sea. After spending their wedding night together, Johann left Martha to join his regiment. On 25 August 1702, Boris Sheremetev captured Marienburg from Sweden. The Russian forces imprisoned the inhabitants and spent three days looting and plundering the town. A Russian soldier sold Martha to a captain,

In spring 1711, Peter launched a campaign against the Ottoman Empire in the Balkans. Following victory over the Swedes at the Battle of Poltava in 1709, the tsar was in a state of euphoria. The Turks were expected to be a walkover. The Russian generals set off accompanied by their wives, children and lovers and the whole campaign had the atmosphere of a holiday outing. On 6 March, on the eve of their departure from St Petersburg, Peter announced that he was marrying Catherine. After wandered up and down the River Pruth in search of the enemy, the Russian army of 38,000 men suddenly found itself surrounded by a Turkish army of 188,000 men. The Russians were forced to negotiate peace terms with the commander of the Turkish army, Grand Vizier Baltaji Mahommed Pasha. On 11 July, they signed a humiliating peace treaty, forfeiting many fortresses and land, yet keeping the army and tsar intact. The Russian side was headed by Baron Peter Shafirov, who was forced to bribe the vizier with large sums of money. When funds ran dry, Catherine offered her jewellery, swinging the negotiations in Russia's favour. In honour of her sacrifice, Peter founded the Order of St Catherine or the Order of Liberation. On 24 November 1714, she became the first woman in history to be awarded this new decoration. Catherine's jewels were the vizier's undoing. When he returned to the Turkish capital, he was beheaded for agreeing to the peace terms. The whole story, however, may be nothing more than legend.

Marriage of His Royal Majesty Peter the First, Autocrat of All the Russias.
Engraving by Andrei Zubov

Peter became increasingly dependent on Catherine. She understood his character and often saved the victims of his rages from punishment and even death. Always calm and unruffled, she shared all the hardships of Peter's life. She was made a lady-in-waiting in 1710, accompanied the tsar wherever he went and bore him eleven children, most of whom died in infancy.

Family Portrait of Peter I. Picture from a snuffbox by Grigory Musikiisky

Nursery.
Summer Palace of Peter I in St Petersburg

who passed her on to Boris Sheremetev. The general ordered her to wash his laundry, when she was spotted by the tsar's confidant, Prince Alexander Menshikov. Sheremetev was forced to present Martha to Menshikov and she entered his service. Menshikov kept her a secret from Peter the Great, allowing her to occasionally meet up with her Swedish husband, who was now a warrant officer. During a heavy drinking session, Menshikov blurted out his secret to Peter. The tsar asked to see Martha and she immediately took his fancy. Although neither tall nor thin, she was a strapping, healthy woman and Peter had recently broken up with Anna Mons. Much to Menshikov's chagrin, Peter took Martha as his lover in 1703. The prince worked the situation in his own favour, however, and his former servant often interceded on his behalf at the court. Peter sent Martha to live in Preobrazhenskoe, where his sister Natalia taught her Russian and court etiquette. Peter's sisters took an immediate liking to his new acquisition.

In 1704, Martha converted to Orthodoxy, taking the name of Catherine Alexeyevna. Her godparents were Peter's half-sister Ekaterina and his son Alexei. During the reign of Catherine I, Russia was governed by a privy council headed by Prince Alexander Menshikov. The empress spent her days amusing herself with a new lover — the handsome and empty-headed Carl Gustaf Löwenwolde. Thanks to her passion for crackers dipped in strong Hungarian wine, she contracted dropsy and her legs swelled up. She spent the last weeks of her life confined to her bed. On 6 May 1727, after two years on the throne, Catherine died of pneumonia. She was buried alongside Peter the Great in the St Peter and St Paul Fortress.

Grand Carriage. Acquired by Peter the Great at Manufactures impériales des Gobelins during his foreign trip (1716–17), it was intended for coronation festivities

Anna and her sister Elizabeth were awarded the titles of "princess" (*tsarevna*) in March 1711 and "heiress" (*tsesarevna*) in December 1721. Peter planned to marry them to European princes in the interests of Russian foreign policy and they were educated with this aim in mind. They learnt reading, writing, embroidery, dancing and etiquette and were provided with libraries of books.

Portrait of Tsarevich Peter Petrovich as Cupid. Artist: Louis Caravaque

Portrait of Tsarevnas Anna Petrovna and Elizabeth Petrovna. Artist: Louis Caravaque

Assembly under Peter I. Artist: Stanislav Khlebovsky

Emperor
Peter II
1715–1730

Parents:
Tsarevich **Alexei Petrovich**
and Princess **Charlotte Christina Sophie
of Brunswick-Wolfenbüttel.**

Peter was born in Petersburg on 12 October 1715. His mother died when he was only ten days old, leaving him in the care of his wayward father. Peter the Great disliked the offspring of his disloyal son and gave the child over to the care of his sister Natalia. After the death of Peter the Great, Prince Menshikov replaced his teachers with the vice chancellor, Ostermann, who left the boy completely to himself. As a result, he never gained anything more than a superficial education. He was a shy and reserved child. Peter was tall for his age and when he was fourteen looked more like sixteen or eighteen.

Peter was particularly enamoured by his beautiful aunt, the charming and temperamental Elizabeth Petrovna. He fell in love with her and several courtiers mooted the possibility of their marriage. This idea collapsed, however, when Elizabeth fell in love with Alexander Buturlin and Peter's love turned cold. After escaping the clutches of Prince Alexander Menshikov, Peter fell under the influence of Prince Alexei Dolgorukov and his son Ivan. At the end of 1727, the court moved to Moscow for Peter's coronation, which was held at the Dormition Cathedral on 24 February 1728. Dim-witted, empty-headed and vain, Ivan Dolgorukov soon became Peter's intimate friend. A lover of alcohol and depravity, he led the young emperor into an exciting new world of physical pleasures and inebriation. Another of Peter's passions was hunting.

Peter II was completely uninterested in affairs of state. He announced that he was an opponent of the transformations of Peter the Great and set about dismantling the institutions founded by his illustrious grandfather. Ivan's father, Prince Alexei Dolgorukov, decided to marry Peter to his daughter Ekaterina and they were officially engaged at Lefortovo Palace in Mos-

On 8 September 1727, Menshikov was put under house arrest. The following day, General Saltykov arrived at his palace with an order for his arrest. The prince and his family were banished to Berezov in Siberia and stripped of their property and decorations. Menshikov, his wife and Peter's prospective bride Maria all died in exile.

Menshikov in Berezov.
Artist: Vasily Surikov

21 October 1727	Signing of the Treaty of Kyakhta with China regulating the Sino-Russian border.

Peter was declared emperor in 1727, at the age of eleven, becoming a puppet in the hands of the grandees. Before she died, Catherine I had written a will of fifteen points, entrusting power to the privy council until Peter reached adulthood. After the empress's death, Menshikov moved the new emperor into his own palace and, on 23 May 1727, announced his engagement to his own daughter Maria, four years his senior. Maria was awarded the Order of St Catherine and the official title of "fiancée and ruling princess." Menshikov was promoted to the ranks of full admiral and generalissimo, while her brother became the only man in Russia to hold the Order of St Catherine, normally only for women, besides the Order of St Andrew. Maria's sisters were awarded the Order of St Alexander Nevsky. When Prince Menshikov was ill for a month with haemoptysis and fever, Peter managed to extract himself from his influence. He was helped by Ostermann, his sister Natalia, the Dolgorukov family and his aunt Elizabeth, all of whom had reasons to dislike Menshikov.

Princess Ekaterina Dolgorukova.
Engraving

Peter II and Elizabeth Petrovna Riding to Hounds.
Artist: Valentin Serov

cow on 30 November 1729. That day, the carriage driving Ekaterina into the palace got stuck in a rut. The golden crown atop the carriage fell off and smashed. Many regarded this as a bad omen. The royal wedding was set for 19 January 1730. On 6 January, during the traditional blessing of the waters on the River Moscow, Peter caught a cold. The following day, he contracted smallpox. The emperor died at Lefortovo Palace on 19 January, the day he should have been married. Histories are generally scathing of the two-year reign of Peter II, forgetting that he was still only a boy. He was buried in the Archangel Cathedral, bringing to an end the male line of the Romanov dynasty.

Empress
Anna Ioannovna
1693–1740

Parents:
Tsar **Ioann V Alexeyevich**
and **Praskovia Fedorovna Saltykova.**

Anna Ioannovna was born in Moscow on 28 January 1693. She grew up with her mother and sisters in Izmailovo outside Moscow. A shy and reserved girl, she studied reading, writing, German, French, dancing and etiquette, but never advanced far beyond the bare essentials of literacy.

Anna grew into a clumsy and gruff young woman. Count Burkhard Christoph von Münnich remembered her physical appearance: "Large and well-shaped, her lack of beauty was compensated by her noble and majestic features. She had large, sharp brown eyes, a slightly longish nose, a pleasant mouth and good teeth. Her hair was dark, her face was freckled and her voice was strong and piercing. She was well-built and never despondent for

View of the Village of Izmailovo.
Engraving by Ivan Zubov

long." Countess Natalia Sheremeteva also described the future empress: "She was frightening to look at and had a repulsive face. She was so large that when she walked between others, she was a head above them. She was also extremely fat." Other contemporaries noted her rough face, great height, dark complexion, clumsy manners, deep voice, slovenliness and many other unattractive features.

In 1709, Peter the Great decided to further Russia's foreign interests by

Countess Natalia Sheremeteva described the future empress: "She was frightening to look at and had a repulsive face. She was so large that when she walked between others, she was a head above them. She was also extremely fat." Other contemporaries noted her rough face, great height, dark complexion, clumsy manners, deep voice, slovenliness and many other unattractive features.

marrying one of his nieces to a European prince. His choice fell on the nephew of King Frederick I of Prussia — Duke Friedrich Wilhelm of Courland. Peter asked his half-brother's widow, Praskovia Fedorovna, which of her three daughters she would prefer to marry to a foreign prince. Praskovia had seen and disliked the duke of Courland, so she chose her least favourite daughter, the seventeen-year-old Anna.

Anna married Duke Friedrich Wilhelm in the still unfinished Menshikov Palace in St Petersburg on 31 October 1710. Peter the Great threw a grand banquet with a great amount of alcohol. The following day, he held a second celebration in honour of the wedding of two dwarves. Peter hoped to breed a race of small people and ordered dwarves to be sent to St Petersburg from all over Russia. Around seventy of them attended the wedding of his own minim, Yekim Volkov, to one of the court dwarves. The two weddings were joined together in a drinking bout lasting several days.

In January 1711, Anna and Friedrich Wilhelm set off for the capital of Courland, Mitawa (now Jelgava in Latvia). On the way there, tired out from the heavy drinking, the duke fell ill and died twenty-five miles from St Petersburg. Anna was a widow two months after her marriage. The duke's body was taken to Courland for burial and his wife returned to St Petersburg.

Peter the Great ordered Anna to return to Mitawa and rule Courland. Realising that his unintelligent niece might not necessarily act in Russia's best interests, the emperor dispatched his lord steward, Peter Bestuzhev-Rumin, who was given three tasks — to govern Courland, to inform the tsar of everything going on there and to be Anna's lover. Her mother protested at the last point, until she was reminded of her own youth, when she had betrayed Tsar Ioann V and given birth to a child fathered by her own bailiff, Vasily Yushkov.

Peter the Great allowed Anna forty thousand roubles a year for the running of her court. This sum was not enough to maintain her position as the ruler of a small European state and the duchess was constantly obliged to ask Peter or his wife Catherine for money. When she was allowed to visit St Petersburg, she also borrowed from Russian aristocrats. In 1726, when Peter Bestuzhev-Rumin was recalled from Courland, Anna fell madly in love with Ernst Johann von Biron. He was an impoverished local nobleman, who had escaped from prison in Königsberg, where he had killed a soldier in a fight.

After the death of Peter II in January 1730, the privy council decided to offer the Russian throne to Anna, with strict limitations on her power. A special list of "conditions" was compiled for Anna to sign. She was not allowed to declare war, make peace, set taxes, spend government money, sign death sentences and distribute or confiscate estates and honours without the permission of the eight-man council. On 25 January 1730, Russian envoys arrived in Mitawa with the document, which Anna signed.

1730	Foundation of two new guards regiments — the Izmailovsky and Horse Guards.
1731	Caucasian territories included in the composition of the Russian Empire.
	Opening of the Military Academy for Noblemen in St Petersburg.
1733–35	War of the Polish Succession.
1733–39	Russo-Turkish War. Russia loses one hundred thousand men, but acquires Azov and the land between the River Bug and the River Dniester. Moldavia comes under Russian protection.
1733–43	The Great Northern Expedition to explore Siberia, the shores of the Arctic Ocean and Kamchatka.
1734	A new government for the Ukraine, consisting of a council of three Russians and three Ukrainians under the control of the Senate.
1735–40	Revolts in Bashkirostan and Kirghizstan (1738).
1736	Introduction of military service lasting twenty-five years.
1738	Opening of the first ballet school in St Petersburg.

Ernst Johann von Biron.
Engraving

Anna Ioannovna was the only purely Russian empress in Russian history. The unintelligent and lazy tsaritsa took virtually no role in the running of the state. She did not even sign the majority of official documents, preferring to leave them to her ministers.

Artyomy Volynsky.
Engraving

Count Burkhard Christoph
von Münnich

Privy councillor
Prince V. Dolgorukov

The new empress hurried to Moscow for her coronation. On 25 February 1730, a group of Moscow noblemen presented her with a petition, asking her to reject the conditions and rule as an autocrat. Anna tore up the document in public and arrested the members of the privy council, who were either sentenced to death or banished. On 28 April 1730, Anna Ioannovna was crowned empress of Russia in the Dormition Cathedral. Although Anna ostensibly ruled Russia with the help of a cabinet of five ministers, she left the running of the state to Ernst Johann von Biron. This period of Russian history was a time of German influence and power abuses, when all the key government posts were held by men of foreign origin. Ironically, Anna Ioannovna was the only purely Russian empress in Russian history. The unintelligent and lazy tsaritsa took virtually no role in the running of the state. She did not even sign the majority of official documents, preferring to leave them to her ministers.

In January 1732, Anna transferred the court back to St Petersburg from Moscow, a city she disliked for its traditional values and customs. After living in relative poverty in Europe, the empress decided to make up for lost time. Foreigners gasped at the splendour of the Russian court and Anna's own passion for luxury. The empress held parties and other forms of wild entertainment involving jesters, dwarves, idiots, Negroes, cripples and Kalmyks. Anna enjoyed watching comedies performed by Italian and German actors. She particularly liked fight scenes and organised similar contests between the court jesters. One of the empress's other passions was card games, in which enormous sums were won and lost. One of her jesters, an Italian fiddler and juggler called Pedrillo, amassed a large fortune and returned to his hometown of Naples. Wild animals were let loose in the Peterhof Park to satisfy Anna's lust for hunting. Loaded rifles stood in all the palace rooms so that the empress could shoot at birds flying past the windows. Anna Ioannovna's love of holding wed-

Empress Anna Ioannovna Tearing Up
the Conditions

Winter Carriage. 1732. Moscow Armoury.
Belonged to Empress Anna Ioannovna

dings for her subjects led to her being termed the "national matchmaker" by one Russian historian. The most famous marriage presided over by the empress was the wedding of one of her jesters, Prince Michael Golitsyn-Kvasnik, to a Kalmyk woman called Avdotia Buzheninova. The event was celebrated in a special house carved from ice on the frozen River Neva.

The empress held parties and other forms of wild entertainment involving jesters, dwarves, idiots, Negroes, cripples and Kalmyks. Anna enjoyed watching comedies performed by Italian and German actors. She particularly liked fight scenes and organised similar contests between the court jesters.

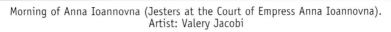

Morning of Anna Ioannovna (Jesters at the Court of Empress Anna Ioannovna).
Artist: Valery Jacobi

All this was paid for by taxing the population. Under Anna Ioannovna, the institution of serfdom was strengthened, with landless peasants being sold like cattle. When people complained, they attracted the attention of the Secret Chancellery of Investigations, who sent the more unruly elements to the block or scaffold.

On 5 October 1740, Anna Ioannovna fainted during lunch. After twelve days of illness, she died of as a result of a kidney stone. The empress was buried in the St Peter and St Paul Cathedral on 23 December 1740. Nine years earlier, on 17 December 1731, Anna signed a manifesto restoring Peter the Great's practice of the sovereign designating his or her own successor. Before her death, she bequeathed the throne to her great-nephew, Ioann Antonovich, who was born in August 1740. Until he reached the age of majority, the country was to be ruled by Ernst Johann von Biron, whom Anna had made duke of Courland in 1737.

Wedding of Jesters in the Ice Palace.
Engraving

View of the Old Winter Palace of Empress Anna Ioannovna from the Admiralty Meadow. Engraving. Artist: Mikhail Makhayev

Regent
Anna Leopoldovna
1718–1746
Emperor
Ioann VI
1740–1764

Parents of Anna Leopoldovna:

Ekaterina Ioannovna, elder sister of Empress Anna Ioannovna and niece of Peter the Great and Duke **Carl Leopold of Mecklenburg-Schwerin.**

Husband:

Prince **Anton Ulrich of Brunswick-Wolfenbüttel**, nephew of the Austrian empress and cousin of Peter II.

Emperor Ioann VI with his mother
Anna Leopoldovna

Elizabeth Catherine Christine was born in Rostock on 7 October 1718. Empress Anna Ioannovna decided to bring her niece up herself. On 12 May 1733, at the age of fourteen, the girl converted to Russian Orthodoxy and took the name of Anna in honour of her aunt. She grew into a graceful and shapely blonde. Although her face gave little away and she often seemed bored, she spent entire days daydreaming or in a state of melancholy. As Empress Anna Ioannovna did not have any children of her own, she decided to marry her niece in an attempt to produce a male heir for the Russian throne. Her choice fell on Prince Anton Ulrich of Brunswick-Wolfenbüttel. They were married in St Petersburg on 3 July 1739. Anna gave birth to Ioann Antonovich, on 12 August 1740.

In March 1762, Peter III visited the fortress in disguise and had a conversation with Ioann lasting many hours. He saw a fair-haired young man of average height with a hooked nose and large eyes. Although he stuttered, Peter observed that "his conversation was intelligent and animated." Peter planned to free Ioann from imprisonment, only he himself was overthrown by his wife Catherine three months later.

When Empress Anna Ioannovna died in October 1740, the throne passed to the two-month-old Ioann with Biron as regent. Biron's regency lasted one month. On the night of 9 November 1740, he was overthrown and exiled to Pelym in Siberia. Uninterested in affairs of state, the regent preferred to leave the government of the country to Ostermann, while she herself spent her time in bed or playing cards. All this set the scene for another palace coup of 25 November 1741, when Elizabeth Petrovna burst into her bedroom with several officers of the guard. Anna and her children were banished to Riga, Dinamund, Rannenburg and, finally, Kholmogory. Ioann was separated from the rest of the family, who did not even suspect that they were all actually living in the same house. He was harshly treated and even not allowed to see a doctor. In 1756, Ioann was transferred to Schlüsselburg Fortress and placed in solitary confinement. Not even the prison governor was told the identity of the prisoner. Elizabeth feared a coup in his favour and set about destroying all papers, coins and anything else depicting or mentioning Ioann. The prisoner was kept in harsh conditions. Daylight was not allowed into his cell and candles were the only source of light. The dungeon was closely guarded and the boy never knew whether it was day or night. The only book he was allowed to read was the Bible. The prison guards noted that his "mental abilities were disturbed ... he stuttered so badly that even those with practice had difficulty understanding him." In August 1762, Catherine II came to the fortress. A deposed emperor was dangerous to a German princess who had seized the Russian throne. Catherine ordered him to be guarded carefully and, in the event of an attempt to free him, to be killed. Ioann VI was secretly buried in an unmarked grave inside the Schlüsselburg Fortress.

The most important events during this short reign were the start of the Russo-Swedish War and the victory of Field-Marshal Peter Lassy at the Battle of Villmanstrand on 23 August 1741. The war ended when Elizabeth Petrovna signed the Treaty of Åbo with Sweden on 18 August 1743, acquiring three Finnish provinces.

On the night of 4/5 July 1764, Vasily Mirovich, a sub-lieutenant of the Smolensk Regiment who served in the garrison, entered the fortress with a small detachment. He attempted to free Ioann, who was instantly put to death by his captors. Although Mirovich was beheaded in St Petersburg on 15 September 1764, there is good reason to believe that his rescue attempt was instigated by Catherine II.

Emperor Peter III Visiting Ioann Antonovich Incognito at the Schlüsselburg Fortress. Artist: Fedor Burov

Silhouettes of the children of Anna Leopoldovna

Empress Elizabeth Petrovna
1709–1761

Parents:
Emperor **Peter I Alexeyevich**
and Empress **Catherine I Alexeyevna.**

Elizabeth Petrovna was born in Moscow on 18 December 1709. She was educated by foreign tutors, who taught her a love of dancing and foreign languages. Besides being fluent in Italian, German and French, she was an excellent dancer and rider.

Elizabeth was officially proclaimed a princess (*tsarevna*) on 6 March 1711 and heiress (*tsesarevna*) on 23 December 1721. Under her mother (Catherine I) and nephew (Peter II), she led a merry and frivolous lifestyle.

Portrait of Anna and Elizabeth, Daughters of Peter I. Unknown Artist

Elizabeth was commonly regarded as the leading beauty of the Russian Empire. Many foreign princes hoped to marry Elizabeth, but the only suitor whom she loved was Carl August, the younger brother of Prince Carl Friedrich of Holstein. He died of smallpox in summer 1727 and Elizabeth never forgot him. She remained forever attached to Holstein and, when she became empress, summoned her nephew Peter to Russia, along with his bride, Sophie of Anhalt-Zerbst, whose mother was Carl August's cousin. Although she never married, Elizabeth had a long line of lovers, including General Alexander Buturlin, lord steward Semyon Naryshkin (her cousin) and a page of the chamber called Alexei Shubin, whom Anna Ioannovna exiled to Siberia in 1732.

As the daughter of Peter the Great, Elizabeth was particularly popular with the guards regiments created by her father. She often visited the regiments, marking special events with the officers and acting as godmother to their children. The guards repaid her kindness on the night of 25 November 1741, when the thirty-two year-old princess seized power with the help of the Preobrazhensky Regiment. Arriving at the regimental headquarters, wearing a breast-plate over her dress and grasping a silver cross, she addressed three hundred grenadiers. Holding up the cross, she asked the men: "Who do you want to serve? Me, the natural sovereign, or those who have stolen my inheritance?" After swearing allegiance to her, kissing her hand and the cross, the troops marched to the Winter Palace, where they arrested the infant emperor, his parents and their own lieutenant colonel, Count von Münnich. It was a daring coup and it passed without bloodshed. Elizabeth had vowed that if she managed to capture the throne, she would not sign a single death sentence as empress.

1741–43	Russo-Swedish War. Treaty of Åbo between Russia and Sweden.
1748	War of the Austrian Succession.
1754	Abolition of internal tolls and customs.
	Foundation of the Nobles Loan Bank.
	Foundation of the border service corps and an institute of customs patrols.
1754–62	Construction of the Winter Palace in St Petersburg.
1755	Foundation of Moscow University.
1756	Foundation of the first Russian public theatre under Fedor Volkov.
1756–62	Russian victories over Prussia in the Seven Years War.
1757	Establishment of the Imperial Academy of Arts in St Petersburg.
1759	Russian victory at the Battle of Kunersdorf.
1760	Russian army captures Berlin.

Accession of Elizabeth Petrovna on 25 November 1741.
Artist: Yevgeny Lanceray

Many foreign princes hoped to marry Elizabeth, among them Prince George of England, Infant Manuel of Portugal, Infant Don Carlos of Spain, Duke Ernst Ludwig of Brunswick, Count Moritz of Saxony and even Shah Nadir of Persia. Fate decreed, however, that she would never marry. The only suitor whom she loved was Carl August, the younger brother of Prince Carl Friedrich of Holstein. He died of smallpox in summer 1727 and Elizabeth never forgot him. She remained forever attached to Holstein...

She kept her word. The following day, a royal manifesto proclaimed a new empress, Elizabeth I, explaining that the preceding reigns had led Russia to ruin: "The Russian people have been groaning under the enemies of the Christian faith, but she has delivered them from the degrading foreign oppression." The population had indeed suffered under a series of German favourites and Elizabeth exiled the most unpopular of them, including Heinrich Johann Friedrich Ostermann, Burkhard Christoph von Münnich and Carl Gustaf Löwenwolde. The new empress was crowned in the Dormition Cathedral on 25 April 1742. During the ceremony, she herself placed the crown on her own head. Elizabeth had no political ambitions of her own and disliked

Catherine Palace in Tsarskoe Selo. 1752–56.
Architect: Bartolomeo Francesco Rastrelli

Amber Room — interior designed by Rastrelli by the order of Elizabeth Petrovna in the Catherine Palace

Bouquet of flowers from precious stones. 1740s. Jeremie Posier, St Petersburg

Elizabeth was commonly regarded as the leading beauty of the Russian Empire. The Duke of Liria wrote: "Princess Elizabeth ... is a beauty the like of which I have never seen. The colour of her face is remarkable. She has flaming eyes, a perfect mouth, the whitest neck and a remarkable body. She is tall and extremely lively. She dances well, rides without the smallest fear and is intelligent and pleasant in conversation." Empress Anna Ioannovna disliked Elizabeth, who kept out of sight during her reign.

governing. Documents often waited months for her signature. When given a treaty with Austria to sign, a wasp settled on the pen and the empress put the quill aside. She only returned to signing the document six months later. She sided against Prussia in the Seven Years War out of her personal dislike of Frederick the Great. Under Elizabeth, St Petersburg was the most dazzling court in Europe. Foreigners were amazed at the luxury of the sumptuous balls and masquerades. The empress adored dancing and new clothes. She issued special decrees governing the styles of the dresses and decorations worn by courtiers. No one was allowed to have the same hairstyle as the empress. Elizabeth owned fifteen thousand ball-gowns,

Snuffbox with Pugs. 1752. Master:
Dmitry Vinogradov, St Petersburg

several thousand pairs of shoes and an unlimited number of silk stockings. She never went to bed before six o'clock in the morning and spent each night in a different room, never having a permanent bedroom. Despite her love of parties and dresses, Elizabeth was extremely religious. She visited convents, made pilgrimages to holy sites and spent long hours in church. When asked to sign a law secularising church lands, she said: "Do what you like after my death, I will not sign it." All foreign books had to be approved by a church censor. Klyuchevsky called her a "kind and clever, but disorderly and wayward Russian woman" who combined "new European trends" with "devout national traditions."

Coronation throne of the Empress
Elizabeth. 1740–42

Suite of State Rooms, known as the Golden Rastrelli Enfilade
in the Catherine Palace

Before she became empress, Elizabeth had fallen in love with Alexei Razumovsky — a handsome member of the court choir. When Elizabeth ascended the throne, she promoted him to chamberlain and the rank of lieutenant general. She is even alleged to have secretly married him in the village of Perovo outside Moscow during her coronation. Although occupying an official position, Razumovsky was never asked to do any work because "Elizabeth wanted to spare him and even published a special decree forbidding anyone from giving him notes or requests."

Vice-chancellor
Count Alexey Bestuzhev-Riumin

View of the Summer Palace of Elizabeth Petrovna from the River Fontanka.
Artist: Alexei Grekov after a drawing by Mikhail Makhayev

Count Alexei Grigoryevich
Razumovsky

In her youth Elizabeth had fallen in love with Alexei Razumovsky. In 1756, Elizabeth made him a field-marshal on his birthday, 17 March, even though he did not know the first thing about military tactics and had never commanded a unit. On his next birthday, 17 March 1757, he was presented with the Anichkov Palace. Elizabeth Petrovna had another intimate friend — Ivan Shuvalov. The son of a guards captain, Ivan Menshoi Shuvalov, and Tatyana Rostislavskaya, he had pleasant manners and a handsome face. Ivan Shuvalov received a good education and knew several European languages. He began his career as a page of the chamber at the court of Grand Duchess Catherine Alexeyevna, who remembers him as a quiet, modest young man whom she often came across with a book in his hands. Ivan Shuvalov fell in love with Princess Anna Gagarina, an intelligent and well-read girl who was eight years his senior. She reciprocated his love and the couple hoped to get married. Ivan's cousins, however, decided that there was more benefit to be

Count Ivan Ivanovich
Shuvalov

Empress Elizabeth Petrovna in Tsarskoe Selo.
Artist: Yevgeny Lanceray

gained from making him the favourite of Elizabeth Petrovna. They prevented the marriage between the twenty-two year-old Ivan and the thirty-year-old Anna and managed to arrange an audience with the forty-year-old empress. Elizabeth took an immediately liking to Ivan Shuvalov. In September 1749, she appointed him gentleman of the bedchamber, followed by the usual posts and titles awarded to all favourites — chamberlain, lieutenant general, adjutant general and knight of the Orders of St Alexander Nevsky and the White Eagle. Elizabeth's ministers attempted to ingratiate themselves with the empress's favourite by offering him even more titles and awards — senator, count and the Order of St Andrew. Shuvalov, however, was not interested. He was happy with his status as the empress's secretary, which gave him access to her at all times. His opinion decided the outcome of all requests and petitions submitted to Elizabeth. Ivan drafted replies to the reports submitted by foreign diplomats and military commanders, writing the texts of Imperial decrees without bearing any legal responsibility for them. Anyone wanting to reach the empress could do so only through Shuvalov.

In 1761, the French diplomat Jean-Louis Favier wrote: "He interferes in

Portrait of Empress Elizabeth Petrovna.
Artist: Georg Caspar von Prenner. Detail

all affairs, although he does not have any special titles or posts ... In short, he enjoys all the advantages of a minister without actually being one."

Elizabeth's health deteriorated in the late 1750s, when she suffered a series of dizzy spells. She refused to take any medicine and became reticent and irritable. She forbade the word "death" to be uttered in her presence.

Elizabeth died in St Petersburg on 25 December 1761 and was buried in the St Peter and St Paul Cathedral on 3 February 1762 after lying in state for six weeks. Her death interrupted the Romanov line. Although all following sovereigns were called Romanovs, they were not Russians.

Sister Dosifeya, believed to be the daughter of Empress Elizabeth and Razumovsky

Emperor Peter III
1728–1762

Parents:

Peter the Great's daughter **Anna Petrovna** and Duke **Carl Friedrich IV of Holstein.**

Wife:

Empress **Catherine II Alexeyevna,** Princess Sophie Friederike Auguste of Anhalt-Zerbst. Married: 21 August 1745.

Peter was born in the city of Kiel in Holstein on 10 February 1728. His mother died when he was three months old and he lost his father when he was eleven. The future emperor of Russia was educated by a marshal of the Holstein court. Bullied and harshly punished for the slightest misdemeanour, the sickly child developed a lifelong hatred of learning.

When Elizabeth Petrovna seized power in 1741, she invited her nephew to St Petersburg to ensure that the throne passed to her father's descendants. Carl Peter Ulrich converted to the Russian Orthodox Church and was proclaimed Elizabeth's heir on 7 November 1742. Peter was horrified at the idea of becoming emperor of Russia. He disliked everything about Russia and this irritated the empress. Elizabeth gave him Russian tutors, but his antipathy towards learning meant that he preferred to spend his time in the company of

King Frederick II of Prussia.
Engraving. Detail

After ruling Russia for 186 days, Peter III was buried in the Annunciation Burial Vault of the St Alexander Nevsky Monastery. Although Catherine II later attempted to portray everything done by Peter III in a bad light, several important projects were nevertheless begun by the emperor and continued by his widow. These include the rebirth of the Russian navy, the abolition of the Secret Chancellery of Investigations, which had struck fear into the population, and a decree freeing the nobility from their obligation to serve the state.

Order of St Anna. Founded in honour of Peter's mother by his father

Grand Duke Peter Fedorîvich and Grand Duchess Catherine Alexeyevna with an Arab. Artist: Anna-Rosina Liszewska

servants. After looking round for a suitable bride, Elizabeth settled on Princess Sophie Friederike Auguste of the minor principality of Anhalt-Zerbst. They were married on 21 August 1745 in St Petersburg. When Elizabeth died in 1761, her nephew ascended the throne as Peter III. This signalled the start of the Holstein-Gottorp-Romanov dynasty, which ruled Russia until 1917. Peter made a disastrous start to his reign by withdrawing Russia from the Seven Years War and concluding peace with his idol, King Frederick II of Prussia, when the Prussians were on the point of suing for peace. All the Russian victories and sacrifices were in vain. Eastern Prussia was returned to Frederick and Russia received no indemnities or compensations. The Russian army seethed with indignation at having to make peace with Prussia and then join a military alliance against their former allies. Peter also made himself unpopular by freeing Münnich, Biron and the other Germans. A plot was soon hatched in St Petersburg to replace Peter with his wife Catherine. She cunningly portrayed herself as the innocent victim of a despotic husband. When one of the conspirators was arrested on 27 June, they made their move. Accompanied by a group of officers and supported by the guards regiments, Catherine arrested Peter on 28 June and declared herself empress. The grandees, dignitaries, courtiers and statesmen all swore a new oath of loyalty to her. On 6 July 1762, Peter III was officially claimed to have died of "haemorrhoidal colic".

Empress Catherine II

1729–1796

Parents:
Prince **Christian August of Anhalt-Zerbst**, commander of a regiment in the Prussian army (later promoted by King Frederick II from major general to the rank of field-marshal) and Princess **Johanna Elisabeth of Holstein-Gottorp.**

Husband:
Emperor **Peter III Fedorovich.**

Children:
Pavel Petrovich (see Emperor Paul I).
Anna Petrovna (1757–1759).

Catherine the Great was born on 21 April 1729 in the town of Stettin (now Szczezin). Catherine's mother, was twenty-two years younger than her husband. She

Catherine Alexeyevna with his son.
Artist: Georg Caspar von Prenner

was a nervy, flighty trouble-maker who did not get on with her husband. The future empress was christened Sophie Auguste Friederike or "Fike" for short. Contemporaries have suggested that her father may have been Frederick the Great or Russian diplomat Ivan Betskoi. The latter theory is supported by the fact that when she became empress, Catherine always kissed Betskoi's hand when she entered the room and allowed him to sit in her presence, when everybody else had to stand. During a phlebotomy, she is alleged to have said: "Let all the German blood flow out of me, so that only the Russian remains."

Sophie Auguste Friederike received a good education at home. She knew French well, spoke Italian and understood English. She enjoyed reading books on history and philosophy. The future empress had a quick brain, a forceful character, pleasant manners and the ability to create a favourable impression on others. Unfortunately, she was tone deaf. People also noted the girl's egoism and ambitious nature.

Catherine II at the Death Bed of Empress Elizabeth Petrovna. Artist: Nikolai Ge

Catherine II with Son and Courtiers on the Balcony of the Winter Palace on 28 June 1762. Watercolour after Johannes Kaestner

On 26 January 1744, Sophie and her mother came to Russia at the invitation of Empress Elizabeth Petrovna to marry the heir to the throne. The first Russian town on their route was Riga, where the princess was met by an escort headed by the legendary story-teller Baron Carl Friedrich Hieronymus von Munchhausen. After converting to the Orthodox Church as Catherine Alexeyevna, she married Peter Fedorovich. After successfully deposing her husband on 28 June 1762, Catherine had herself crowned empress at the Dormition Cathedral on 22 September 1762. Ironically, the reign of this German princess brought more benefit to Russia than under her native-born predecessors. Although Catherine left the Russian finances in a perilous state and the country in a state of disorder, she took care to create the image of a great ruler. Her reign is often regarded as the "golden age of Catherine". While paying tribute to many of her undoubted

1763	Opening of orphanages in St Petersburg and Moscow.
1764	Creation of the Hermitage art collection. Abolition of the post of Cossack hetman in the Ukraine. Secularisation of church lands. Opening of the Smolny Institute for Noble Girls in St Petersburg. Vasily Mirovich's attempt to free Ioann VI from the Schlüsselburg Fortress ends in the murder of the ex-tsar.
1765	Foundation of the Free Economic Society.
1765	Annexation of the Aleutian Islands.
1768–75	Russo-Turkish War.
1768	Foundation of the Assignation Bank. Printing of paper money. Vaccinations against smallpox.
1769	First foreign loan floated in Amsterdam. Foundation of the Order of St George.
26 June 1770	Defeat of the Turkish fleet at the Battle of Çesme.
1771	Plague riots in Moscow.
1772, 1793 and 1795	Partitions of Poland, bringing White Russia, Volhynia, Podolia, Lithuania and Courland.
1773–75	Revolt lead by Yemelian Pugachev.
21 July 1774	Treaty of Küçük Kaynarca between Russia and Turkey.
1775	Liquidation of the Zaporozhian Host. Introduction of serfdom in the Ukraine.
1780	Declaration of "armed neutrality" to guarantee "freedom of trade and navigation".
1781	Austro-Russian alliance.
27 September 1782	Foundation of a special customs force to prevent the illegal import and export of goods.
1782	Foundation of the Order of St Vladimir.
1783	Opening of the Russian Academy for the Study of the Russian Language Treaty of Georgievsk places eastern Georgia under Russian protection. Annexation of the Crimea.
1784	Assimilation of Alaska.
21 April 1785	Charter to the Nobility granting the status of a legal entity to the nobility and the right to elect a marshal in each province and Charter to the Towns granting a limited degree of corporate self-administration.
1787–91	Russo-Turkish War.
1788–90	Russo-Swedish War.
3 August 1790	Treaty of Värälä between Russia and Sweden.
9 January 1792	Treaty of Jassy between Russia and Turkey.
1793	Foundation of Odessa.
1794	Uprising in Poland led by Thaddeus Kosciuszko.

Catherine tried hard to be a real Russian tsaritsa. She studied the Russian language, although she never lost her accent, closely observed Orthodox traditions and even introduced Russian national dress at the court. She wrote: "I owe everything to Russia, even my name!" During a phlebotomy, she is alleged to have said: "Let all the German blood flow out of me, so that only the Russian remains."

Books from the library of Catherine II.
Second half of the 18th century

Lomonosov Showing Catherine II his own Mosaic Works in his Study.
Artist: Alexei Kivshenko

successes, however, her role in Russian history should not be exaggerated. Andrei Bolotov wrote that "under the all-powerful Prince Potemkin, for several years, we had only one recruitment

Peacock Clock. 18th century.
Mechanic: James Cox, England

The Winter Palace.
The State (Jordan) Staircase

Catherine nevertheless had a European upbringing and a Western mind. She corresponded with enlightened French philosophers and seriously considered introducing their ideas into Russia. The empress enjoyed hunting, horse-riding, dancing, balls and other forms of entertainment.

... and absolutely everything was embezzled by the prince and his minions and favourites." The conscripts were often plundered and turned into private property. Alexander Bezborodko claimed that in 1795 as many as fifty thousand men were missing from an army of four hundred thousand.

By the end of Catherine's reign, the Russian army was in a sorry state. General Langeron observed sadly: "All you have to do to become a cavalry officer in Russia is to be able to ride a horse." Andrei Bolotov wrote: "In the guards regiments, the sub-colonels and majors did what they liked. Even the secretaries were ready to confer ranks on anyone for money. Service in the guards was an out-and-out comedy." The Preobrazhensky Regiment alone numbered several thousand warrant officers and sergeants. With the full knowledge of the commanders, secretaries accepted bribes for including noblemen, merchants, clerks, apprentices and priests

Battle of Çesme on 26 June 1770.
Artist: Jakob Philipp Hakkert

Statue of Voltaire.
Sculptor: Jean-Antoine Houdon

Tsarskoe Selo.
Panorama of the Catherine Palace and Parks

in the regiment. The official lists included infants and sometimes even unborn children — before the sex of the baby was even known. None of these people served, but simply lived in their houses or estates, advancing from rank to rank. Upon reaching the position of over-officer, they transferred to the army, where they were promoted another two ranks — without knowing the slightest thing about military service.

Unlike such other Russian empresses as Anna Ioannovna or Elizabeth Petrovna, for whom favourites were merely a whim, Catherine elevated the practice to a state institution. She herself claimed to be doing the state a service by educating and promoting talented young men. The results of this form of "education" varied. Although she twice bore children to her favourites, they were more than just lovers, of which Catherine had many.

Presenting a Letter to Catherine II.
Artist: Ivan Miodushevsky

Portrait of Catherine II with
the Text of an Order. Enamel miniature

Things were little better in the civil service. Towards the end of Catherine's reign, eleven thousand cases lay unanswered in the Senate. The bureaucracy was riddled with corruption. Nothing could be done without paying a bribe. Catherine's wars exhausted the exchequer. Money was not backed by gold and there was a large public deficit. The prices of such essential foodstuffs as bread and salt rose sharply, hitting the poor hardest. In the countryside, landowners chopped down forests for firewood, without bothering to plant new trees. Many other negative phenomena flourished in Russia under Catherine. Catherine had a talent for finding the right people for the right job. She was extremely able in her choice of statesmen — and lovers. The same man sometimes performed both roles. The institution of favourites flourished under Catherine. The em-press spent enormous sums of money on her lovers (historians have calculated that they cost Russia the exact sum of 95.5 million roubles). She generously presented crown peasants to her lovers and other favourites, increasing the total number of serfs in the country. The empress gave away a total of 800,000 heads.

Besides her successor, Grand Duke Paul, Catherine also bore Grigory Orlov a son in 1762, who was known as Alexei Bobrinsky. In 1775, she bore Grigory Potemkin a daughter called Elizabeth Temkina.

Towards the end of her life, Catherine was often ill. Her legs swelled up and she died of a brain aneurysm on 6 November 1796. She was buried in the St Peter and St Paul Fortress.

Snuffbox with Set of Precious Stones. Circa 1790.
Master: P. M. G., St Petersburg. Detail

Catherine II Walking in Tsarskoe Selo.
Artist: Vladimir Borovikovsky

Favourites of Catherine II:
Count Grigory Orlov
Prince Grigory Potemkin
P. Zavadovsky
S. Zoritch
I. Rimsky-Korsakov
A. Lanskoy
A. Dmitriev-Mamonov
Prince Platon Zubov

Emperor Paul I
/1754–1801/

Parents:
Emperor **Peter III Fedorovich**
and Empress **Catherine II Alexeyevna.**

Wives:

Natalia Alexeyevna, Princess Auguste Wilhelmine Luise of Hesse-Darmstadt (1755–1776). Married: 29 September 1773.

Maria Fedorovna, Princess Sophie Dorothea Auguste Luise of Württemberg. (1759–1828). Married: 26 September 1776.

Children of Paul and Maria Fedorovna:

Alexander (see Alexander I).

Konstantin (1779–1831). Catherine II hoped that one day he would reclaim Constantinople from the Turks. Ruler of the kingdom of Poland and commander-in-chief of the Polish army (1814). Known for his harshness and unbalanced character. Coined the expression "war spoils a soldier." Married a Polish countess, Johanna Grudna-Grudczinska, who became known as the Most Serene Princess Lowicka. This morganatic marriage deprived Konstantin of his right to the Russian throne, a fact never made public, leading to confusion in 1825 and the December Revolution. Died of cholera in Vitebsk on 15 June 1831. Buried in the St Peter and St Paul Fortress. Had two illegitimate children with French actresses.

Alexandra (1783–1801). When she was thirteen, Catherine II decided to marry her to King Gustav IV of Sweden. The king agreed, then changed his mind, enraging the empress.

Elena (1784–1803). Married Grand Duke Friedrich Ludwig of Mecklenburg-Schwerin.

Maria (1786–1859). Married Grand Duke Carl Friedrich of Sachsen-Weimar-Eisenach. Friend of Goethe.

Ekaterina (1788–1819). Rejected Napoleon's offer of marriage (1807). Married Duke Peter Friedrich Georg of Oldenburg.

Olga (1792–1795).

Anna (1795–1865). Rejected Napoleon's offer of marriage (1809). Married the future King William II of Holland (1816). Queen Beatrice of Holland is her great-great-granddaughter.

Nikolai (see Nicholas I).

Mikhail (1798–1849). Married Princess Friederike Charlotte Marie of Württemberg (1806–1873), a great-niece of Empress Maria Fedorovna, who converted to Orthodoxy as Grand Duchess Elena Pavlovna. Elena gave birth to five daughters.

Paul was well-read and had an excellent knowledge of French and literature. He also studied Slavonic, German, history, geography and mathematics. The future emperor was physically strong, interested in art, polite, well-mannered and enjoyed jokes. He was extremely religious, abhorred debauchery and highly rated nobility and honesty.

Grand Duke Paul Petrovich as a child

Grand Duke Paul Petrovich

Paul was born in St Petersburg on 20 September 1754. In 1760, Paul began his education under Nikita Panin. One of the best minds in Russia, Panin had studied all the latest teaching methods. His mother deprived him of the rights and privileges normally associated with this title. She kept him well away from the throne, in a state of virtual banishment. He sat and bided his time, observing the surrounding lawlessness. On 29 September 1773, Paul married Princess Auguste Wilhelmine Luise of Hesse-Darmstadt, who converted to Orthodoxy on 14 August 1773 as Grand Duchess Natalia Alexeyevna. She died giving birth in April 1776 and was buried in the St Alexander Nevsky Monastery. Paul married another German princess on 26 September 1776. This was Princess Sophie Dorothea Auguste Luise of Württemberg, who converted to Orthodoxy on 14 September 1776 as Grand Duchess Maria Fedorovna. She bore him four sons and six daughters, died in 1828 and was buried alongside her husband in the St Peter and St Paul Cathedral.

When Paul eventually inherited the throne in 1796, he attempted to turn the country around. His first step was to summon all guardsmen to their regiments, which brought several surprising details to light. Most officers had deserted their regiments for their country estates or villages, where they had also enlisted their children, whose ages were often given as eighteen when they were in fact not even ten. The entire country was in a state of flummox. Thousands of officers hurried to their regimental headquarters, increasing transport costs and leading to further grumbling among the nobility. Guardsmen were

Exercise-book of the Grand Duke Paul Petrovich. 1759

1796	Creation of new guards regiments — Hussar Life Guards, Cossack Regiment and Artillery Battalion and the Cavalry Guards (1800).
	Reburial of Peter III.
1797	Decree on the inheritance of the throne.
	Introduction of three-day husbandry service for serfs.
	Foundation of the Russian cavalier order.
1798	Prohibition of the sale of landless house servants and serfs.
	Paul is elected grandmaster of the Order of St John of Jerusalem.
1798–99	War with France. Suvorov's campaigns in north Italy and Switzerland and Admiral Ushakov's victory in the Mediterranean Sea (1799).
1801	Planned invasion of British India.
	Annexation of Georgia.

Portrait of Paul I as Grand Master of the Order of Hospitalers (Knights of St. John of Jerusalem). Artist: Vladimir Borovikovsky

Throughout his life, Paul was haunted by rumours that his father was Count Saltykov, that Catherine II was not his mother or that Elizabeth Petrovna had substituted a Finnish peasant child for Catherine's still-born baby. These rumours were inspired by Catherine herself, in order to consolidate her own hold on the throne. Portraits of Peter III and Paul clearly reveal the physical similarities between father and son.

Grand Duchess Natalia Alexeevna,
first wife of Paul I

Chess. 1760s. Kholmogory.
Unknown master

Books with Paul's ex-libris.
Late 18th century

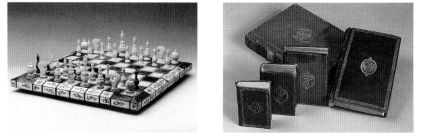

wrote: "In the offices, departments and ministries, everywhere in the capital, the candles were already lit at five o'clock in the morning. All the chandeliers and fireplaces blazed in the vice chancellor's mansion opposite the Winter Palace, while the senators sat round their red table at eight o'clock." Corruption at the highest levels was harshly punished.

In an attempt to combat inflation, five million paper roubles were burnt outside the Winter Palace. The enormous palace services of silver were melted down and turned into coins. Loaves were sold from special crown storehouses in an attempt to reduce the cost of bread. The price of salt was lowered and decrees were issued on the protection of forests and the prevention of fires. The Russo-American Company was established to start trade with the United States. A school of medicine was founded in St Petersburg. Paul passed an incredible number of new laws — 595 in 1797, 509 in 1798, 330 in 1799, 469 in 1800.

Pavlovsk Palace.
Picture Gallery

Portrait of Maria Fedorovna.
Artist: Alexander Roslin

banned from wearing fur coats or muffs, as this was not part of their uniform. Paul introduced a new uniform costing twenty-two roubles. To avoid freezing in cold weather — the average temperature in St Petersburg in February 1799 was minus 37°C — officers wore woollen sweaters beneath their jackets or lined the jacket with fur.

Paul addressed other areas of Russian life, including the bureaucracy. Civil servants were expected to earn their pay honestly. As one contemporary

Insignia and star of the order
of St John of Jerusalem

Paul had a vexed relationship with his mother, whose coup had led to the death of his father. He became the heir to the throne at the age of seven and remained so for the next thirty-five years.

Paul's throne. 1797. St Petersburg.
Master Christian Mayer

The emperor was determined to drag Russia out of the state of stagnation into which it had fallen during the "golden age of Catherine." Unlike his mother, however, he lacked the ability to choose the right people. Much progress was nevertheless made. The Credit Bank lent large sums of money to the nobility. Russia led the world in the production of pig iron, smelting 155,000 tons in 1800. The Old Believers were allowed to practise and build their own churches. Paul is often criticised for his decree of 18 April 1800 limiting the import of foreign literature. In the words of the new law, "corruption of the faith, civil laws and morality is being spread by various books imported from abroad. We therefore command, to the point of a decree, the prohibition of various imported books, no matter what language they are written in ... and works of music." Paul was no democrat. He was the sovereign of the country and regarded the morality of his subjects as his personal responsibility. This was not a complete ban, merely a recommendation "to the point of a decree". Russia was flooded with foreign literature, much of it of dubious content, and the emperor did not want his people to read or listen to works corrupting their minds and souls.

In international relations, Paul was forced to resolve a series of difficult problems. On his way to Africa, Napoleon

Gatchina Palace.
Paul's Throne Room

Paul passed a series of reforms designed to improve the Russian army. He introduced individual frontline training and attempted to combat abuses by commanders. Russian military historian Sergei Panchulidze writes: "Many of Paul's innovations still survive today, with great benefit to the army. Taking a dispassionate look at his military reforms, one cannot deny that the Russian army is greatly indebted to him."

landed on Malta, expelled the Russian ambassador and promised to sink any Russian ship daring to approach the island. As Paul had taken Malta under his personal protection, he regarded this hostile act as a declaration of war and joined the anti-French alliance in 1798. Under pressure from his allies, Austria and Britain, he placed Alexander Suvorov at the head of the Russian army. Suvorov hatched an ambitious plan to single-handedly defeat the two French armies in north Italy and to march from there on Paris.

Alexander Suvorov's plan was thwarted by the treachery of the Austrians. After defeating the French armies in north Italy, Austria demanded that Suvorov join up with the forces of General Alexander Rimsky-Korsakov in Switzerland, despite the difficult climatic conditions and the lack of any help from Russia's ally. When Suvorov's army arrived in Switzerland, they found that Rimsky-Korsakov had already been defeated by the French. The Russians were without provisions or supplies and surrounded by a numerically superior French army. The French were better

Review of Troops near St Michael's Castle under Paul I.
Artist: Alexander Benois

equipped and supplied and had the experience of mountain warfare. With great difficulty, Suvorov managed to extract himself from Switzerland by crossing through the Alps. He took ill on the road back to St Petersburg and died soon after his arrival in the Russian capital. The crossing of the Alps is nevertheless still regarded as one of the finest chapters in the history of the Russian army.

Angry at Austrian and British perfidy, Paul decided to change sides. Watching Napoleon destroy the last vestiges of the French Revolution in his desire to become emperor, he joined France in an anti-British alliance. Russia's task was to march on the English colonies in India. In January 1801, Paul ordered Fedor

Emperor
Paul I

Paul I and the Escort of Honour Rendering a Salute to Maria Fedorovna.
Artist: O. Gottlieb

St Michael's Castle. 1784–1800.
Architects: Vasily Bazhenov, Vincenzo Brenna

St Michael's Castle.
South facade

Orlov-Denisov, hetman of the Cossacks, to prepare to invade India: "All the riches of India will be your reward ... My maps only go as far as Khiva and the River Amudarya. Beyond there, it is your duty to get information from the English and their Indian subjects." Paul's murder two months later, however, meant that the planned invasion of India never took place.

Paul was murdered in his palace bedchamber on the night of 11/12 March 1801. The plot was led by two former favourites of Catherine, the Zubov brothers, with the alleged support of the British government, alarmed at the alliance between Russia and Napoleon. Paul was buried in the St Peter and St Paul Fortress.

The Family of Paul I.
Artist: Gerhard von Kügelgen

Pieces from the Guriev Service.
St Petersburg

Emperor Alexander I
1777–1825

Parents:
Emperor **Pavel I Petrovich** and Empress **Maria Fedorovna.**

Wife:
Elizabeth Alexeyevna, Princess Luise Marie Auguste of Baden (1779–1826). Married: 9 October 1793.

Children:
Maria Alexandrovna (1799–1800). Grand Duchess.
Elizabeth Alexandrovna (1806–1808). Grand Duchess.

Alexander was born in St Petersburg on 12 December 1777. He was raised in Spartan conditions and, as a result, never fell ill. Catherine II personally supervised the education of Alexander and his younger brother, Konstantin,

Portrait of Alexander and Konstantin.
Artist: Richard Brompton

laying out her instructions in a special document entitled *Instructions for the Education of my Grandsons.* The boys were taught by Frédéric César de la Harpe, who was later one of the directors of the Helvetic Republic under Napoleon Bonaparte. Alexander grew up reticent, suspicious and conceited. He was known for his clever mind, diplomacy and indecisiveness. When he heard of the plot against his father, he did not take any precautionary measures. Ascending the throne, he merely banished the ringleaders from St Petersburg.

The first half of Alexander's reign was a period of moderate and liberal reforms. The emperor relied upon the help of such young friends as Prince Adam Chartoryisky, Count Pavel

1801	Annexation of Georgia.
1802	Colleges replaced by ministries.
1803–06	First Russian round-the-world voyage by Ivan Krusenstern and Yury Lisyansky.
1804–13	Russo-Persian War.
1805–07	Russia joins the anti-Napoleonic alliance.
1806–12	Russo-Turkish War.
	New guards regiments — Jäger Regiment, Guard Equipage, Lithuanian and Finnish Dragoon Regiments, Black Sea Company.
1808–09	Russo-Swedish War.
1810	Formation of the State Council.
1811	Foundation of the Tsarskoe Selo Lyceum.
1812–14	War with Napoleonic France.
1815	Poland is absorbed into the Russian Empire.
1815–26	Round-the-world trip of Otto von Kotzebue.
1816	Start of the Caucasian War.
1819	Opening of St Petersburg University.
1820	Fabian Gottlieb von Bellinshausen and Mikhail Lazarev discover the Antarctic.
1822	Banning of Masonic lodges.

Personal books of Alexander I
decorated with the imperial cipher. Early 19th century

Portrait of the Emperor Alexander I.
Artist: Franz Krüger

Stroganov, Count Victor Kochubei and Count Nikolai Novosil-tsev. Together, they formed the Unofficial Committee, which issued manifestos restoring the charters of Catherine II to the nobility and towns, granting pardons to those who had suffered under the previous tsar and allowing the purchase and sale of land by all free individuals. New universities were opened in Kharkiv, Kazan, Derpt and Vilno. Existing educational establishments were awarded new freedoms. The result was a renaissance of many aspects of Russian life. One of the most famous institutions founded by Alexander I was the Tsarskoe Selo Lyceum in 1810. Many famous Russians were educated there, including the poet Alexander Pushkin. When he was a lyceum student, Pushkin paid tribute to Alexander's role in the war against Napoleon and the liberal reforms at the start of his reign. The growing conservatism of the tsarist regime, however, forced the poet into the arms of the opposition. When this criticism crept into his writings, Pushkin was banished from St Petersburg. After that, he was generally negative in

Juvenile suit of Grand Duke
Alexander Pavlovich. 1784

Alexander grew up reticent, suspicious and conceited. He was known for his clever mind, diplomacy and indecisiveness. When he heard of the plot against his father, he did not take any precautionary measures. Ascending the throne, he merely banished the ring-leaders from St Petersburg.

Mantel clock with the figure of Julius Caesar. Circa 1811. Paris

his appraisals of Alexander's personality and policies. Before then, however, he had lauded what he called the "wonderful first days of Alexander."

One of the most important symbols of the changes taking place in Russian life under Alexander was Mikhail Speransky (1772–1839). The son of a priest in Vladimir Province, he studied at seminaries in Vladimir and St Petersburg. Metropolitan Gabriel recommended Speransky to Prince Alexei Kurakin, who employed him as his secretary.

Portrait of Empress Elizabeth Alexeyevna. Unknown artist

Tsarskoe Selo.
Catherine Palace. Alexander I Study

Grand (Stone) Theatre.
Unknown artist. After 1818

•••••• 1812

Napoleon's attack spurred Alexander into action. He declared that he would not lay down arms until every last enemy soldier had been expelled from Russian soil. The tsar vowed never to sign peace, not even if he had to retreat to the end of the Russian Empire: "It is I or Napoleon; we cannot exist together."

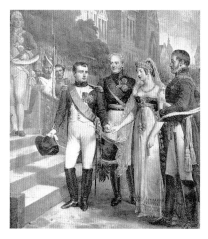

Napoleon and Alexander I in Tilsit.
Artist: Nicholas Gosset

Emperor Alexander I and Emperor Napoleon in Tilsit Chasing in Ettersberg, in the Outskirts of Weimar. Artist: Ilya Repin

He stayed with Kurakin when the latter was appointed general procurator by Tsar Paul. Under Alexander, he was transferred to the Ministry of the Interior. When the minister of the interior fell ill, he asked Speransky to deliver his reports to the tsar. Alexander took a liking to Speransky and, in 1808, invited him to draw up a liberal constitution based on West European models, with the foundation of a state council and parliament or *duma*. Speransky never succeeded in implementing his programme. The indecisive tsar was frightened by the hostility of the nobility to his liberal reforms. Unable to win over the aristocracy and court circles, he sacrificed Speransky to appease the opposition. Speransky was accused of plotting with Napoleon and exiled to Perm. Thanks to the intercession of Count Alexei Arakcheyev, Speransky was appointed governor of Perm in 1816 and governor general of Siberia. In 1821, he was returned to St Petersburg and made a member of the State Council. After the December Revolution of 1825, Speransky sat on the special court of investigation and passed the sentences. The rest of his life was spent compiling *Complete Collection of the Laws of the Russian Empire*, for which he was awarded the Order of St Andrew and the title of count. In 1805, Russia was drawn into the anti-Napoleonic wars, ending with the humiliating Treaty of Tilsit. This was followed by wars against Turkey and Sweden and the French invasion of 1812.

Alexander I.
Artist K. Shevelkin

Emperor Alexander I Meeting People Headed by Priests on the Road to Smolensk on 11 July 1812

127

The Battle of Borodino was fought on 26 August 1812. Both sides suffered heavy losses, with 44,000 Russians and 58,000 Frenchmen killed. In the evening, after reviewing the situation, Fieldmarshal Mikhail Kutuzov gave the order to retreat.

Kutuzov during the Battle of Borodino.
Artist A. Shepeliuk

ary 1813, the French were finally thrown out of Russia. Alexander and his army pursued Napoleon throughout Europe, eventually entering Paris in 1814. The emperor often rode into the field of battle himself. At the Battle of Lutzen in 1813, advised to retreat to a safe distance after coming under heavy fire, he replied: "My bullet is not here." Although the French had plundered and pillaged in Russia,

Last Hours of Borodino.
Artist: Victor Vereschagin

Napoleon in the Moscow Kremlin.
Artist: Victor Vereschagin

Emperor Alexander I and Grand Duke Konstantin Pavlovich

Napoleon's attack spurred Alexander into action. He declared that he would not lay down arms until every last enemy soldier had been expelled from Russian soil. The tsar vowed never to sign peace, not even if he had to retreat to the end of the Russian Empire: "It is I or Napoleon; we cannot exist together." When the Grand Armée occupied Moscow and the city caught fire, Alexander regarded this as a divine punishment for his sins and his role in his father's murder. On 7 Janu-

Angel atop the Alexander Column situated at the centre of Palace Square in St Petersburg

The unexpected death of the emperor and the nocturnal funeral among close friends gave rise to many myths. The most popular legend is the claim that Alexander did not die and someone else was buried in his place. The sovereign retreated to Siberia, later resurfacing as Fedor Kuzmich, a *starets* (monastic spiritual leader) known for his righteous life who died in January 1864.

Paris escaped the same fate. On 10 April 1814, Alexander ordered an Orthodox Easter mass to be celebrated in the spot where King Louis XVI had been guillotined. He was gracious towards the ex-empress Josephine and her children. At the Château de Malmaison, the Russian emperor acquired the collection of paintings belonging to Napoleon's first wife for the Imperial Hermitage.

After the Hundred Days, when Napoleon escaped from Elba and attempted to regain power, the Russian army reoccupied Paris. The tsar was welcomed by the local population and on 25 April 1814, the Russian State Council, Holy Synod and Cabinet of Ministers awarded him the title "Alexander the Blessed". This was followed by the Congress of Vienna and the post-war reconstruction of Europe.

These heady events and the lingering pangs of conscience over his father's murder led Alexander to increasingly immerse in mysticism. While the peasants were herded into

military settlements, pseudo-religious and mystical cults flourished throughout the country. Russia entered yet another period of stagnation. Alexander was a handsome and charming man. Napoleon wrote home to Josephine: "Were he a woman, I would probably fall in love with him." The tsar had a beautiful wife to match — Princess Luise Marie Auguste of Baden (1779–1826). She converted to Orthodoxy as Grand Duchess Elizabeth Alexeyevna and they were married on 9 October 1793. Elizabeth was a niece of the first wife of Paul I. She gave birth to two daughters, who both died in infancy. Alexander soon lost interest in his wife and took a string of

Starets
Fedor Kuzmich

mistresses. The longest affair was with Maria Naryshkina (née Chetvertinskaya), who gave birth to several of his children. Alexander I died in Taganrog on 19 November 1825. He was buried in the St Peter and St Paul Cathedral on 13 March 1826. Two months later, his wife died and was buried alongside him. The unexpected death of the emperor and the nocturnal funeral among close friends gave rise to many myths. The most popular legend is the claim that Alexander did not die and someone else was buried in his place. The sovereign retreated to Siberia, later resurfacing as Fedor Kuzmich, *starets* (in Eastern Orthodoxy, a monastic spiritual leader) who died in a forest near Tomsk in January 1864.

Palace of Alexander I
in Taganrog

Interior of the monastic cell of Fedor Kuzmich in a forest near Tomsk

Emperor
Nicholas I
1796–1855

Parents:

Emperor **Pavel I Pavlovich** and Empress **Maria Fedorovna.**

Wife:

Alexandra Fedorovna, the daughter of Frederick William III of Prussia, Princess Fredericke Luise Charlotte Wilhelmine (1798–1860). Married: 1 July 1817.

Children of Nicholas I and Alexandra Fedorovna:

Alexander Nikolaevich (see Alexander II).

Maria Nikolaevna (1819–1876). Educated by the poet Vasily Zhukovsky, she wept when she heard of the death of Alexander Pushkin. Maria was known for her beauty, grace, charm, fine manners and strong character. She married Maximilian Eugene Joseph August Napoleon de Beauharnais, duke of Leuchtenberg and one of the cleverest and most handsome princes in Europe. Although they had seven children, Maria and Maximilian did not have a happy marriage.

Olga Nikolaevna (1822–1892) married Crown Prince Friedrich Alexander of Württemberg in Peterhof on 13 July 1846, who became King Karl I in 1864.

Alexandra Nikolaevna (1825–1844) married Landgraf Friedrich Wilhelm of Hesse-Kassel on 28 January 1844. She died giving birth to a still-born son, Wilhelm, in Tsarskoe Selo.

Konstantin Nikolaevich (1827–1892) was educated by Admiral Fedor Lütke. He was an admiral (1831), member of the State Council, and naval minister (1855–81). Reformed the Russian navy, building new ships powered by steam. Contributed to the reforms of Alexander II (1860s). Ruler of the kingdom of Poland (1862–64), where he survived an assassination attempt. Chairman of the State Council (1865–81). Withdrew from public life after the accession of Tsar Alexander III (1881). Married Princess Alexandra Friederike Henriette of Sachsen-Altenburg (Grand Duchess Alexandra Josifovna).

Nikolai Nikolaevich (1831–1891). Served in the Russian army, though not noted for his abilities as a commander. Married Princess Alexandra Friederike Wilhelmine of Oldenburg (Grand Duchess Alexandra Petrovna).

Mikhail Nikolaevich (1832–1909) was chairman of the State Council (1881–1905). Supported conservative groups of the nobility. Married Princess Cäcilie Auguste of Baden (Grand Duchess Olga Fedorovna).

Dish presented to Emperor Nicholas I. 1831. Moscow.
Masters *С. Ж.* and *В. С.*

Uprising on 14 December 1825 on Senate Square
in St Petersburg. Artist: Carl Collmann

Nicholas was born in Tsarskoe Selo on 6 July 1796, the last year of the reign of Catherine II. The empress described her impressions of her third grandson: "He is two feet in length, with arms no shorter than mine and a deep bass voice. I have never seen such a cavalier. If he continues to grow, his brothers will be dwarves in comparison with this colossus. Although he has two elder brothers, I believe that he is destined to rule." Nicholas was educated first by a Scottish nurse, Jane

Nicholas I and his Retinue.
Artist: Franz Krüger

IMPORTANT EVENTS

1826	Foundation of the Third Department or secret police.
1826–28	Russo-Persian War ending with the signing of the Treaty of Turkmanchai on 10 February 1828, giving Russia part of Persian Armenia.
8 October	Victory of Admiral Mikhail Lazarev over the Turko-Egyptian fleet at the Battle of Navarin.
1828–29	Russo-Turkish War ending with the signing of the Treaty of Adrianopole (2 September 1829), giving Russia part of the eastern shore of the Black Sea, the Akhaltsikhski Pashalyk and the mouth of the Danube.
1830–31	Popular uprising in Poland.
23 June 1831	Cholera riots in St Petersburg. Nicholas addresses a crowd of five thousand people on Senate Square and calls for an immediate end to the disorders.
1832	Foundation of the Military Academy.
1833	Pavel Schilling invents the world's first electromagnetic telegraph.
	God Save the Tsar (music by Alexei Lvov and words by Vasily Zhukovsky) adopted as the national anthem.
1834	Opening of St Vladimir University in Kiev.
	Yefim and Miron Cherepanov build the world's first railway at the Lower Tagil Factory in the Urals.
1835	Compilation of the *Code of Laws of the Russian Empire*, covering over thirty thousand laws in forty-five volumes.
1837	Opening of a railway line between St Petersburg and Tsarskoe Selo.
17 December 1837	Fire destroys the inside of the Winter Palace.
1838	Boris Jacoby invents the process of electroforming.
1839	Opening of the Nicholas (Pulkovo) Astronomical Observatory.
	Abolition of the Uniate Church in the Ukraine and White Russia.
1848	Police surveillance of the universities and students going abroad.
1849	Russian forces led by Count Ivan Paskevich of Erivan, Prince of Warsaw, crush the Hungarian revolution. The Russian action is widely condemned in Western Europe.
1851	Opening of the Nicholas Railway between St Petersburg and Moscow.
1852	Opening of the New Hermitage, designed by German architect Leo von Klenze.
1853	General Vasily Perovsky captures the Kokand fort of Ak-Mechet (now Kzyl-Orda) on the River Syr Darya in Central Asia.
1853–56	Crimean War. Britain, France and Sardinia inflict a series of defeats on Russia.
1855	Treaty of peace and friendship with Japan.

Like the great commanders of the past, Nicholas led a Spartan lifestyle. He slept on an iron camp bed under an army overcoat and ate simple food. Such personality traits as a love of order and discipline betray the soldier in Nicholas. Although he could be harsh with his subordinates, he always tried to be fair. As a result, the future emperor was respected, rather than loved. Practical and realistic, he worked eighteen hours a day, amazing contemporaries with his stamina.

Victory of Admiral Mikhail Lazarev over the Turko-Egyptian fleet at the Battle of Navarin on 8 October 1827. Unknown artist

Portrait of Nicholas I. Artist: Franz Krüger

Commemorative medal dedicated to the Cathedral of Christ the Saviour

View of the Cathedral of Christ the Saviour. Rebuilt in 1990s

Lyon, and then by General Lamsdorf. The general was not particularly intellectual and used traditional teaching methods. His best way of getting his point across was to rap his pupil across the knuckles with a ruler or ramrod. Nicholas developed a dislike for abstract ideas and only brightened up when his lectures came to an end and he was allowed to engage in war games. As he

was not expected to inherit the throne, Nicholas's education was limited to military and engineering disciplines. On 14 January 1822, Tsar Alexander I signed a secret manifesto, making Nicholas the heir to the throne. Not even Nicholas himself knew of the existence of this document. When the news of Alexander's death in Taganrog reached St Petersburg on 27 November 1725, he immediately swore an allegiance of loyalty to his elder brother, Konstantin. The State Council, Senate and army did the same. At the same time, in Warsaw, Konstantin and the kingdom of Poland swore an oath of allegiance to Nicholas. When the confusion was eventually cleared up, the whole country prepared to take a new oath of allegiance to Emperor Nicholas I on 14 December 1825. That day, on Senate Square, several regiments refused to swear the oath to Nicholas. The tsar acted promptly and decisively. He surrounded the rebels with loyal forces and gave the order to open fire on them. The December Revolution was harshly suppressed. Five of the ringleaders were executed, while 120 active participants were exiled or sentenced to hard labour. The soldiers and

Nicholas I was more than just a limited man married to the army. He was an excellent draughts-man and, like another famous military commander, Frederick the Great of Prussia, played well on the flute. He attended the opera and ballet, danced well at court balls, enjoyed jokes, liked women and was a moderate drinker. Tall and stately, with a handsome, classical face, the emperor was extremely imposing. A contemporary wrote that he was "more German than Slav." This is nothing to be surprised at, as by this time, the Romanovs were only Russian in name.

Review of troops on the occasion of the victory in the military campaign in Poland on 6 October 1831 on the Tsarina's Meadow (now Field of Mars, St Petersburg). Artist: Grigory Chernetsov

Battle of Sinop. 18 November 1853.
Artist: Alexei Bogoliubov

Admiral Vladimir Kornilov.
Unknown artist

The Slav blood in the Romanov veins was further diluted in 1817, when another German princess joined the Imperial family. Nicholas married the daughter of King Frederick William III of Prussia, Princess Fredericke Luise Charlotte Wilhelmine (1798–1860), who converted to Orthodoxy as Grand Duchess Alexandra Fedorovna. The granddaughter of Frederick the Great was taught Russian by the poet Vasily Zhukovsky.

Episode from the Emperor's Domestic Life.
Artist: Alexei Chernyshev

Winter Palace. Malachite Drawing Room.
Detail of the interior

sailors who had joined the rebellion were subjected to corporal punishment and sent to fight in the Caucasus. Nicholas was crowned in the Dormition Cathedral in Moscow on 22 August 1826. This was followed by a second Polish coronation in Warsaw on 12 May 1829. For his help in suppressing the December Revolution, Nicholas made Count Alexander Benkendorf the head of the Russian police. He promoted him to the rank of cavalry general and awarded him the Order of St Andrew. Benkendorf was entrusted with such delicate tasks as acting as the

Winter Palace.
Malachite Drawing Room

Winter Palace.
Boudoir

Portrait of Empress Alexandra Fedorovna.
Unknown artist

Princesses Maria and Olga.
Artist: Timoleon Neff

intermediary between the tsar and Alexander Pushkin (their extensive correspondence still survives). Between 1826 and 1829, Count Benkendorf kept the poet under close surveillance at the personal request of the emperor. Nicholas's behaviour on Senate Square in 1825 was not the only example of his personal bravery. On 23 June 1831, during cholera riots in St Petersburg, he went out alone to an angry crowd of several thousand people, demanding an immediate end to the disorders. He was equally courageous when the Winter Palace caught fire in December 1837, helping to put out the flames and save the palace property.

Nicholas's slogan was "autocracy, orthodoxy, nationality." His reign marked the heyday of absolute monarchy in Russia. Non-Russian nationalities were subjected to an intense policy of russification and christianisation. The Old Believers were persecuted. The nobility was given preference in everything. Censorship was increased. Almost the entire state budget was spent on the bureaucracy and army.

Nicholas's authoritarianism led to a cult of lies, sycophancy and hypocrisy. Distrusting the bureaucratic apparatus, he extended the powers of his own chancellery, which controlled the main branches of the administration, replacing the higher state organs. Defeat in the Crimean War led to the collapse of Nicholas's system and his own sudden death on 2 March 1855. Although he officially died of pneumonia, there were rumours that he had committed suicide or was poisoned. The tsar was buried at the St Peter and St Paul Cathedral.

Pieces from the Tea Service.
Circa 1854

Emperor Alexander II

1818–1881

Parents:

Emperor **Nicholas I Pavlovich** and Empress **Alexandra Fedorovna.**

Wife:

Maria Alexandrovna, Princess Maximiliane Wilhelmine Auguste Sophie Marie of Hesse-Darmstadt (1824–1880). Married: 16 April 1841.

Children of Alexander II and Maria Alexandrovna:

Alexandra (1842–1849).

Nikolai (1843–1865). Educated by Count Sergei Stroganov. Engaged to Princess Dagmar of Denmark. Died of tubercular meningitis in Cannes.

Alexander (see Alexander III).

Vladimir (1847–1909). He was an infantry general, member of the State Council, president of the Imperial Academy of Arts and honorary member of the Imperial Academy of Sciences. He married Princess Marie Alexandrine Elisabeth Eleonore of Mecklenburg-Schwerin (1854–1920). The daughter of Grand Duke Friedrich Franz II of Mecklenburg-Schwerin and a great-niece of Empress Alexandra Fedorovna, his wife was known as Grand Duchess Maria Pavlovna. She headed the Imperial Academy of Arts after her husband's death.

Alexei (1850–1908). As an admiral general and naval minister, he was responsible for the Russian defeat at the Battle of Tsushima (1905) and was relieved of all his posts (2 June 1905). Died in Paris.

Maria (1853–1920). She married Queen Victoria's second son, Prince Alfred Ernest Albert of Great Britain.

Sergei (1857–1905). He was the governor general of Moscow and commander of the Moscow Military District. Sergei was assassinated by a Socialist Revolutionary on Senate Square in the Moscow Kremlin (17 February 1905). His remains were transferred to the Novospassky Monastery (1995). He married Princess Elisabeth of Hesse-Darmstadt (1864–1918), sister of Empress Alexandra Fedorovna.

Pavel (1860–1919). He was the honorary chairman of the National Health Society. He married his third cousin, Princess Alexandra of Greece (1870–91), who died giving birth to their second child. After marrying a divorced commoner, Olga Karnovich, he was dismissed from his posts and obliged to live abroad. Returning to Russia before the start of the First World War, he was shot by the Bolsheviks in Petrograd.

Alexander II was born in Moscow on 17 April 1818. He was brought up bearing in mind that one day he would inherit the throne. He received a good education under Carl Merder, a battle officer, and the poet Vasily Zhukovsky. Besides Russian, the tsarevich also knew French, German, English and Polish. He studied mathematics, physics, geography, history, political economy, statistics and law and developed a taste for art. At the age of nineteen, Alexander and Zhukovsky embarked on a long journey across Russia. He was the first member of the Imperial family to visit Siberia, where he met several of the exiled Decembrists and managed to improve their living conditions. The tsarevich spent the following years travelling round Europe. Alexander was known for his kind heart, geniality, quick mind,

1855	Russo-Japanese treaty of peace and friendship.
18 March 1856	Treaty of Paris ending the Crimean War.
26 August 1856	Foundation of the Tretyakov Gallery, later donated to the city of Moscow (1892).
1856–57	Peter Semyonov's expedition to Tien-Shan.
3 January 1857	Creation of the Secret Committee to overhaul the system of serfdom.
11 April 1857	Confirmation of the coat of arms of the Russian Empire.
1857	Formation of a national system of customs organs.
	Peasant disorders in western Georgia.
1858	Annexation of the Amur territories and Pacific coast.
1859	Conquest of the eastern Caucasus.
4 March 1859	Start of work of commissions on the abolition of serfdom.
31 May 1860	Foundation of the State Bank.
1861	Abolition of serfdom.
12 May 1862	Passing of temporary rules on the press.
1862	Opening of the St Petersburg Conservatoire.
18 June 1863	New education statute giving wide autonomy to the universities.
26 June 1863	New law on crown peasants.
1863–64	Uprisings in Poland and Lithuania.
1 January 1864	New law on provincial and district institutions.
1864	Conquest of the western Caucasus.
	Reform of the departments of foreign trade and tax collection at the Ministry of Finance.
	New law on primary schools and statute on grammar schools.
	Reform of the legal and court system.
1865	Implementation of the temporary rules on the press.
	Reform of the military court system
	Capture of Tashkent.
1867	Sale of Russian America to the United States.
1868	Capture of Samarcand and Bukhara.
17 February 1869	Dmitry Mendeleyev discovers the periodical table of elements.
1870–82	Nikolai Miklukho-Maklai's journey round Oceania.
1870–88	Nikolai Przhevalsky's expedition to China, Mongolia and Tibet.
1873	Creation of League of Three Emperors between Russia, Germany and Austria.
1 January 1876	Introduction of nationwide military service.
1876	Annexation of Kokand.
1877–78	Russo-Turkish War. Treaty of San Stefano (19 February 1878).
1878	Congress of Berlin.

Grand Duke Alexander
Nikolaevich

Tsarevich
Alexander Nikolaevich

good memory and soft character. When Théophile Gautier visited Russia in 1865, he described the emperor: "The sovereign's short hair frames a high and handsome forehead. His facial features are remarkably correct and might have been carved by an artist. His blue eyes stand out against his brown face, tanned by the wind during long journeys. The outlines of the mouth are as delicate and refined as a Greek sculpture. His majestic, calm and soft facial expression is occasionally set off by a gracious smile." Alexander demonstrated his bravery when he served in the Caucasian army and helped to repulse an attack by wild tribesmen. He was awarded the Order of St George (fourth class) for his heroism.

At an early age, Nicholas I introduced his son to the running of the government, assigning him various administrative posts. In 1842, when the emperor left St Petersburg for a month, he left his son in command. These periods of deputising gradually grew longer and longer.

Alexander succeeded to the throne on 18 February 1855 and was crowned in the Dormition Cathedral in Moscow on 26 August 1856. Along with the throne, he inherited a whole

At an early age, Nicholas I introduced his son to the running of the government, assigning him various administrative posts. In 1842, when the emperor left St Petersburg for a month, he left his son in command. These periods of deputising gradually grew longer and longer.

Coronation of the Empress.
Chrome lithograph by Mihály Zichy

Portrait of Vasily Zhukovsky — Tutor of Grand Duke Alexander Nikolaevich

Tsarevich Alexander Nikolaevich Fighting against Chechens on 26 October 1850.
Woodcut by Nikolai Karazin

series of problems. After losing the Crimean War, Russia was forced to sign the Treaty of Paris, forfeiting a number of possessions and the right to keep a fleet on the Black Sea. The war had revealed the country's economic and political backwardness. Reforms were urgently needed in every area of public life. The implementation of these reforms required not only brains and knowledge, but also an iron will. Unfortunately, this was something that Alexander lacked.

The first reform was a manifesto emancipating the serfs on 19 February 1861. What now looks like a handsome gesture in fact horrified the vast majority of peasants. In order to own any land, they had to buy it from the landowner. Yet their only source of income was from toiling the land. The result was a vicious circle. Although freed from the landowners, agricultural labourers now became dependent on the peasant commune. The landowners also suffered as a result of the reforms. Deprived of a free source of labour, many decided to sell their land to the emerging middle class. The proceeds were either invested in stocks and shares or drunk away. The result was many personal and family tragedies. The land reform of 1864 envisaged self-government at the district and provincial levels. Here too there were prob-

After losing the Crimean War, Russia was forced to sign the Treaty of Paris, forfeiting a number of possessions. The war had revealed the country's economic and political backwardness. Reforms were urgently needed in every area of public life. The implementation of these reforms required not only brains and knowledge, but also an iron will. Unfortunately, this was something that Alexander lacked.

Leonardo da Vinci Room in the Winter Palace. 1858–60.
Architect: Andrei Stackenschneider

Emperor Alexander II
in his study. 1870

lems. The organs of self-government — land councils and the Zemstvo — were riddled with bribery and corruption. Funds were embezzled and rural schools, hospitals, roads and bridges were either built badly or not built at all.

The judicial reforms passed in November 1864 introduced trial by jury. The new juries reached some astonishing conclusions, such as the decision to acquit Vera Zasulich, who had shot and wounded Fedor Trepov, the governor of St Petersburg. The municipal self-government (1870) and military reforms (1874) also had a difficult passage.

Many sections of the population opposed the reforms and enemies of the tsar appeared on both the right and left wings. The peasants were particular disgruntled. The liberalisation of public life led to the emergence of several terrorist organisations whose aim was to kill the emperor. Supported by public opinion, the revolutionaries declared war on the tsar. They made a series of assassination attempts, the last of which was successful.

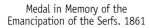

Medal in Memory of the
Emancipation of the Serfs. 1861

Alexander II enjoyed mixed success in international affairs. He brought the Caucasian War to an end (1864) and annexed a series of territories, including the Amur Provinces (1858), Ussuriisk (1860), Turkestan (1867), Emirate of Bukhara (1868), Khiva (1873) and Kokand. Japan recognised Russia's right to southern Sakhalin and the Kuril

Surrender of Pleven (Wounded Osman Nuri Pasha
before Alexander II). Artist: Alexei Kivshenko

Despite his initial love for his wife, Alexander entered into a long-term liaison with one of her ladies-in-waiting — Princess Ekaterina Dolgorukova (1847–1922). While Maria was still alive, she bore him four children — Georgy, Olga, Boris and Ekaterina. Shortly after his wife's death, Alexander married Ekaterina and even considered making her empress.

Empress
Maria Alexandrovna

Princess Ekaterina Dolgorukova with
her Dog in St Petersburg. 1870s

Islands (1876). On the other hand, Alaska and the Aleutian Islands were virtually given away to the United States (1867). Instead of the triumphant entry of Russian forces into Constantinople, Russia only acquired insignificant territories in Bessarabia and Asia Minor as a result of the Russo-Turkish War (1877–78). The pro-German foreign policy brought no real benefit to Russia.

On 16 April 1841, Alexander married Princess Maximiliane Wilhelmine Auguste Sophie Marie of Hesse-Darmstadt (1824–1880). The daughter of Grand Duke Louis II of Hesse-Darmstadt, she converted to Orthodoxy on 5 December 1840 as Grand Duchess Maria Alexandrovna. Alexander and Maria made

Emperor Alexander II
and family. 1870

Many sections of the population opposed the reforms and enemies of the tsar appeared on both the right and left wings. The peasants were particular disgruntled. The liberalisation of public life led to the emergence of several terrorist organisations whose aim was to kill the emperor. Supported by public opinion, the revolutionaries declared war on the tsar. They made a series of assassination attempts, the last of which was successful.

Assassination of 1 March 1881. Alexander II Emerging from his Carriage after the First Terrorist Attack. 1881

Alexander II on his Death Bed. 1881. Artist: Konstantin Makovsky

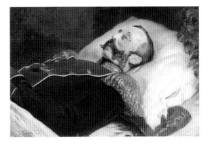

an excellent couple, with his high spirits and her kindness and piety. They had eight children. Maria won much respect in Russia for her charity work, but constantly suffered from poor health. She died of tuberculosis at the age of fifty-five and was buried in the St Peter and St Paul Fortress in 1880. On 1 March 1881, when he was driving along the Catherine Canal, Alexander was killed in a bomb attack. He was buried alongside Maria in the St Peter and St Paul Fortress on 15 March 1881. A church was built on the site of his murder — the Church of the Resurrection of Christ (Church of the Saviour on Spilt Blood).

Church of the Resurrection of Christ (Church of the Saviour on Spilt Blood). Architects: Alfred Parland and Archimandrite Ignatius

Canopy over the Site of the Mortal Wounding of Emperor Alexander II

Emperor
Alexander III
1845–1894

Parents:

Emperor **Alexander II Nikolaevich** and Empress **Maria Alexandrovna**

Wife:

Maria Fedorovna, Princess Marie Sophie Frederikke Dagmar of Denmark (1847–1928). Married: 28 October 1866.

Children of Alexander III and Maria Fedorovna:

Nikolai Alexandrovich (see Nicholas II).

Alexander Alexandrovich (1869–1870).

Georgy Alexandrovich (1871–1899) was the heir to the throne after the accession of Nicholas II (1894). He died of tuberculosis.

Tsarevich Alexander and Alexei with a Goat Cart. Artist: Woldemar Hau

Xenia Alexandrovna (1875–1960) married her third cousin Grand Duke Alexander Mikhailovich.

Mikhail Alexandrovich (1878–1918) was the heir to the throne between Georgy's death (1899) and the birth of Nicholas's son Alexei (1904). He commanded the Wild Division and the Second Cavalry Corps during the First World War (1914–17) and was made a lieutenant general (1916). Married Natalia Sheremetevskaya (1912). He refused the throne after the abdication of Nicholas II (1917) and was shot by the Bolsheviks in Perm (1918).

Olga Alexandrovna (1882–1960) married Duke Peter Friedrich Georg of Oldenburg (1901). After divorcing him, she married Nikolai Kulikovsky (1916). She emigrated after the revolution and died in Canada.

Tsarevich Alexander Alexandrovich
in London. 1870s

Alexander III was born in St Petersburg on 26 February 1845. He was educated by Boris Perovsky, a former head of the Communication Engineers. The grand duke's other tutors were such leading Russian scholars as Jacob Grot, Baron Modest Korf, General Mikhail Dragomirov and Konstantin Pobedonostsev. Alexander received a good education and knew German, French and English. His favourite writer was Mikhail Lermontov and he learnt to play the French horn.

The sudden death of his elder brother Nikolai on 12 April 1865 meant that Alexander was now the heir to the Russian throne. He acquitted himself well during the Russo-Turkish War (1877–78), when he commanded the Ruschuksky detachment and was awarded the Order of St George (second class).

Alexander became emperor of Russia after the assassination of his father in 1881. He was crowned in Moscow on 15 May 1883, a date he preferred to forget, rather than celebrate: "I do not consider that day a holiday and do not accept any congratulations."

Alexander inherited the throne at a difficult time for Russia. One half of society was discontented at the slow pace of

1881	Capture of Ashkhabad.
6 June 1881	Renewal of the League of Three Emperors.
28 December 1881	Lowering of redemption payments and compulsory purchase of peasant plots.
24 June 1882	First flight of an aeroplane designed by Alexander Mozhaisky.
1882	Foundation of the Peasant Land Bank.
	Abolition of the poll tax.
	New factory laws.
	Temporary rules on the press.
1883	Georgy Plekhanov founds the *Emancipation of Labour* group in Geneva.
1884	New university statutes abolishing the autonomy of the universities.
	Introduction of church schools in rural parishes.
1885	Foundation of the Nobles Land Bank.
	Final annexation of Central Asia.
	Morozov Mill Strike.
	Russo-Afghan border conflict.
	Annexation of Merv.
6 June 1887	Signing of Russo-German treaty in Berlin.
12 June 1888	Opening of the first Siberian university in Tomsk.
1889	Village communes brought under closer control by the introduction of the institution of land commandant and the abolition of the office of elected justice of the peace.
12 June 1890	Reform of rural assemblies reducing the influence of the peasants and giving greater weight to the votes of the nobility.
1891	Start of construction of the Trans-Siberian Railway (completed 1905).
1891–92	Famine on the Volga.
1892	Limitations on rural and urban self-government.
	Secret Franco-Russian military alliance.
	New customs laws.
1893	Tariff war with Germany.

On 28 October 1866, Alexander married his tenth cousin, Princess Marie Sophie Frederikke Dagmar of Denmark. Before then, she had been the fiancée of his elder brother Nikolai, who died in 1865. Dagmar converted to Orthodoxy as Grand Duchess Maria Fedorovna. Small, elegant and charming, Maria Fedorovna was the complete opposite of Alexander. She adored balls, which he abhorred. She was an accomplished rider, while he feared horses. One of their few points of common interest was a love of painting.

Polonaise in St Nicholas's Hall of the Winter Palace. Early 1860s.
Artist: Mihály Zichy

Emperor Alexander III and Empress Maria Fedorovna. 1890. Artist: Ivan Kramskoi

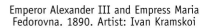

reforms, while the other half feared change. The Russian economy had still not recovered from the war with Turkey. The widespread terror unleashed by revolutionaries had led to the formation of a counter-revolutionary group of monarchists called the Holy Militia. For security reasons, Alexander III was obliged to live away from the capital in Gatchina, where the royal palace had an underground passage leading to the park. From there, he set

about restoring law and order in Russia. The emperor introduced a series of harsh security measures on 14 August 1881. This was followed by laws designed to ease the life of the peasantry. The tsar lowered redemption payments and the compulsory purchase of peasant plots

Imperial train crash at Borki.
17 October 1888

Service of Thanksgiving for the Salvation at Borki. Artist: Ivan Makarov

Dedication to Emperor Alexander III.
Drawing in the Byzantine style

(1881), founded the Peasant Land Bank (1882) and abolished the poll tax introduced by Peter the Great (1886). He regulated working conditions in factories, limiting the hours worked by women and children (1882).

Alexander III transformed other areas of Russian life, provoking discontent among many sections of the population. The intelligentsia condemned the new university statutes, abolishing the autonomy of the universities (1884). They also condemned the decision of Count Ivan Delyanov, minister of education, to prohibit the "children of servants, laundresses and cooks" from studying at grammar schools (1888).

One of Alexander's most popular reforms was a new version of the law on the

Family
of Tsar Alexander III. 1880s

Gatchina Palace park. Birch house.
State room

Portrait of Empress Maria Fedorovna.
Artist: Vladimir Makovsky

Although German in blood, Alexander III was Russian in character. He was physically strong and deeply religious. The emperor did not like lies, flattery, gossip, ceremonies or long speeches. In his private life, he was modest and simple.

Alexander III Examining Troops near Tiflis.
Artist: François Roubau

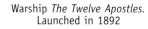

Warship *The Twelve Apostles*.
Launched in 1892

Imperial family, limiting the number of grand dukes on the civil list (2 July 1886). The emperor firmly adhered to the principle of "Russia for Russians" and strengthened the power of the administration.

Alexander III
Artist: Vladimir Makovsky

In foreign policy, Alexander III broke with the Triple Alliance of Germany, Austria-Hungary and Italy and sought a rapprochement with France. In 1892, Russia signed a military alliance with France to counterbalance German aggression in Europe, providing many years of peace and stability on the continent. Personally, Alexander believed that Russia only had two allies — her army and navy — and that the other European nations were not interested in a strong and powerful Russia. The emperor was independent in his dealings with foreign kings. Once, when fishing at Gatchina, an aide-de-camp informed him that an important telegram had arrived from Europe. Alexander replied: "While the Russian tsar is fishing, Europe can wait." By skilful diplomacy, he managed to raise Russia's prestige on the international arena, while maintain-

Room of Grand Duke Alexander Alexandrovich, Commander of the Ruschuksky Detachment in Brestovitsa. Artist: Vasily Polenov

The emperor was independent in his dealings with foreign kings. Once, when fishing at Gatchina, an aide-de-camp informed him that an important telegram had arrived from Europe. Alexander replied: "While the Russian tsar is fishing, Europe can wait."

Throne of Alexander III in the Gatchina Palace.
Second half of the 19th century

ing law and order inside his own borders. For this, the tsar was known as the "peace-maker".

Although German in blood, Alexander III was Russian in character. He was physically strong and deeply religious. The emperor did not like lies, flattery, gossip, ceremonies or long speeches. In his private life, he was modest and simple.

Alexander III cultivated the Russian school of painting. He was a connoisseur of art and collected pictures by Russian masters (mostly Realist painters). The Russian Museum was founded at his initiative and awarded the collection of national painting in the Imperial Hermitage. Before the revolution, the Russian Museum carried his name.

On 28 October 1866, Alexander married his tenth cousin, Princess Marie Sophie Frederikke Dagmar of Denmark. Before then, she had been the fiancée of his elder brother Nikolai, who died in 1865. Dagmar converted to Orthodoxy as Grand Duchess Maria Fedorovna.

Small, elegant and charming, Maria Fedorovna was the complete opposite of Alexander. She adored balls, which he abhorred. She was an accomplished rider, while he feared horses. One of their few points of common interest was a love of painting. The empress was an accomplished artist and several of her works are now in the collections of Russian museums.

Alexander was an exemplary father. He was deeply attached to his wife, whom he called "Minnie". Maria Fedorovna bore him six children. When he died, she fell into a dead faint. The empress managed to escape from Russia after the revolution, dying in Denmark in 1928 at the age of eighty-one. She spent fifty-two years of her life in Russia.

In 1888, the Imperial train crashed near Borki in Kharkiv Province. The tsar held up the mangled roof of the carriage, so that his family could escape from the wreckage. In doing so, he damaged his kidneys. On 2 November 1894, Alexander III died at the age of forty-nine in Livadia in the Crimea. He was buried in the St Peter and St Paul Cathedral.

Alexander III
on his Death Bed

Statue of Alexander III on Znamenskaya (Holy Sign) Square in St Petersburg. Sculptor: Prince Paolo Trubetskoi

Emperor Nicholas II
1868–1918

Parents:
Emperor **Alexander III Alexandrovich** and Empress **Maria Fedorovna.**

Wife:
Alexandra Fedorovna, Princess Victoria Alix Helena Louise Beatrice of Hesse-Darmstadt (1872–1918). Married: 14 November 1894.

Children:

Olga Nikolaevna (1895–1918). Grand Duchess.

Tatyana Nikolaevna (1897–1918). Grand Duchess.

Maria Nikolaevna (1899–1918). Grand Duchess.

Anastasia Nikolaevna (1901–1918). Grand Duchess.

Alexei Nikolaevich (1904–1918). Tsarevich.

Nicholas, Alexandra and their children were exiled to Ekaterinburg, where they were shot on the night of 16/17 July 1918.

Nicholas II was born at Tsarskoe Selo on 6 May 1868. He received a good education at home and was read a special course of lectures between 1885 and 1890. His tutors included Konstantin Pobedonostsev (procurator of the Holy Synod), Nikolai Bunge (minister of finance), Nikolai Girs (minister of foreign affairs), generals Mikhail Dragomirov and Nikolai Obruchev, historian Vasily Klyuchevsky and composer and military engineer Cesar Cui. The teachers never actually learnt how well their pupil had understood their lectures, however, for they were not allowed to ask him any questions, while he himself never asked any. Nicholas also served as an officer at army camps near St Petersburg. Count Sergius Witte wrote that he had the "education of an average guards colonel from a good family."

In 1890, Nicholas alarmed his parents by beginning a love affair with a ballet dancer. The object of his desire was Mathilde Kschessinska, whom he continued to see right up until his engage-

Tsarevich Nicholas
Alexandrovich. 1872

Tsarevich Nicholas
Alexandrovich. 1870s

Nicholas Alexandrovich.
St Petersburg. 1886

ment to Princess Victoria Alix Helena Louise Beatrice of Hesse-Darmstadt in 1893. Alexander III decided to combat his infatuation by sending Nicholas on a long voyage round the world. The tsarevich would sail through the Mediterranean Sea and Suez Canal to India and Japan, before landing at Vladivostok, where he would disembark and return through Siberia to St Petersburg.

The trip was carefully planned by Nicholas's parents to give him a lesson in diplomacy. Recommendations were sent to the Russian ambassador or governor of the places he would visit, describing in detail what could be seen and what should not be seen. Alexander III even drafted the welcoming speeches read to his son. Nicholas was accompanied by his younger brother, Georgy, who suffered from tuberculosis. The two brothers were close in age and their parents hoped that the sun and sea air would restore Georgy's health. They were joined by other young men from good families, including Prince Baryatinsky (suite general), Prince Obolensky (Horse Guards Regiment), Prince Kochubei (Cavalry Guards) and Prince Ukhtomsky (Department of Foreign Confessions).

On 23 October 1890, Nicholas and his companions boarded the *Memory of Azov* and set sail for Athens, where they were joined by Prince George of Greece. The royal party stopped at Egypt to visit the Suez Canal and the pyramids. On board the ship, they spent most of their time indulging in the traditional entertainment of all

1895	Alexander Popov invents the radio telegraph.
1896	Signing of a Sino-Russian alliance against Japan and construction of the Chinese Eastern Railway Line.
1896	Rapprochement with Bulgaria.
1897	First national census.
	New laws regulating working hours.
	Introduction of a new unit of currency — the gold rouble.
1898	Sino-Russian convention leasing the Liaotung Peninsula and Port Arthur to Russia.
1898	Nicholas II calls for an end to the armaments race and initiates two peace conferences at The Hague (1899, 1907).
1900–03	Economic crisis.
1902	Government committees report on the urgent need for radical change in the tsarist administration, finances, economy and local self-government, but its conclusions are ignored.
1904–05	Russo-Japanese War following Russia's refusal to withdraw troops from Manchuria after suppressing the Boxer Rebellion. The war reveals the military backwardness of Russia and leads to a wave of unrest throughout the country, the loss of several territories in the Far East and the sinking of the Russian navy at the Battle of Tsushima.
1904–07	Signing of the Triple Entente between Britain, France and Russia.
9 January 1905	Bloody Sunday and the start of the 1905 revolution.
17 October 1905	October Manifesto granting civil freedoms and a parliament or Duma.
1906–11	Peter Stolypin's agricultural reforms.
19 August 1906	Introduction of military courts to combat the wave of revolutionary terror.
9 November 1906	Decree allowing the government to pass laws in the intervals between Duma sessions.
1907–14	Sergei Diaghilev's *Saisons Russes* in Paris and London.
3 May 1908	School reforms and the introduction of compulsory free primary education.
4 April 1914	Uryankhai region (Tuva) comes under the protection of Russia.
1 August 1914	Germany declares war on Russia.
6 August 1914	Austria-Hungary declares war on Russia.
August 1914	St Petersburg is renamed Petrograd.
October 1914	Russia declares war on Turkey.
27 February 1917	February Revolution and the overthrow of the tsarist regime.

Back in the Russian capital, Nicholas continued his relationship with Mathilde Kschessinska. Although not blessed with long legs, she had beautiful eyes and was a talented dancer. She came from a family of famous ballet dancers and was the first Russian ballerina to master thirty-two consecutive fouettés. With her technical skill and excellent connections inside the Imperial family, Kschessinska quickly became the prima ballerina of the Mariinsky Theatre.

Mathilde Kschessinska.
1900

Members of Coburg royal family.
Coburg, 1894

Tsarevich Nicholas Alexandrovich
in Livadia. 1890s

officers. During one drinking session, Georgy fell and hurt his chest, aggravating his illness. His parents advised him to land at the nearest port and return to Russia. He died of consumption in 1899.

In April 1891, the *Memory of Azov* entered the old Japanese capital of Kyoto. From there, the company travelled to the small town of Otsu, where an attempt was made on Nicholas's life. A policeman ran up and struck him on the head with his sword, just above the right ear. The assailant raised his sword to strike again, but Nicholas jumped out of the rickshaw in which they were travelling, while everyone else turned and fled. Prince George of Greece came to the rescue, knocking the policemen down with his stick and holding him until reinforcements arrived.

Nicholas's parents ordered him to immediately return to Russia. Travelling through Siberia to St Petersburg, he made a stop at the town of Tobolsk, where he would later spend nine months as a prisoner of the revolutionary government.

Back in the Russian capital, Nicholas continued his relationship with Mathilde Kschessinska. Although not blessed with long legs, she had beautiful eyes and was a talented dancer. She came from a family of famous ballet dancers and was the first Russian ballerina to master thirty-two consecutive fouettés. With her technical skill and excellent

Mathilde Kschessinska in Marius Petipa's
ballet *La Fille du Pharaon*. 1898

On 23 October 1890, Nicholas and his companions boarded the *Memory of Azov* and set sail for Athens, where they were joined by Prince George of Greece. The royal party stopped at Egypt to visit the Suez Canal and the pyramids.

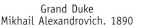

Tsarevich Nicholas Alexandrovich. 1890

Grand Duke Mikhail Alexandrovich. 1890

Tsarevich Nicholas Alexandrovich and his Retinue visiting the Egyptian pyramids. 1891

connections inside the Imperial family, Kschessinska quickly became the prima ballerina of the Mariinsky Theatre.

After Nicholas married Princess Alix of Hesse-Darmstadt, Kschessinska took up with Grand Duke Sergei Mikhailovich, who was responsible for the Russian artillery and the theatrical society. Russians joked: "Thanks to the grand duke, we have a fine ballet and a terrible artillery."

Kschessinska's next admirer was Grand Duke Andrei Vladimirovich — despite a seven-year age difference. In 1902, she gave birth to a son called Vladimir, who was given an hereditary title and the surname Krasinky by the tsar. His original patronymic was Sergeyevich ("son of Sergei") as Mathilde was at that time the common-law wife of Grand Duke Sergei. After marrying Grand Duke Andrei in France in 1921 and converting from Catholicism to Orthodoxy in 1925, Vladimir's patronymic was changed to An-

Tsarevich Nicholas Alexandrovich (fifth from the left) during his round-the-world trip. 1891

Memory of Azov on which Tsarevich Nicholas Alexandrovich made his round-the-world trip. 1890

dreyevich ("son of Andrei"). Kschessinska died in Paris in 1971, a few months short of her hundredth birthday.

Before ascending the throne, Nicholas commanded a battalion of the Preobrazhensky Life Guards. He also acquired experience in government by attending the sittings of the State Council and Cabinet of Ministers and heading the Trans-Siberian Railway Construction Committee.

Nicholas became emperor of Russia on 21 October 1894 and was crowned on 14 May 1896. During the coronation celebrations, 1,300 people were crushed to death and tens of thousands were injured in a stampede for souvenirs at Khodynka Field outside Moscow. Khodynko was the first in a long line of bloody events during the reign of Nicholas II. It was followed by the Russo-Japanese War (1904–05), Bloody Sunday (9 January 1905), the crushing of an armed uprising in Moscow (December 1905), revolutionary terror, police retribution, Jewish pogroms or-

Nicholas Alexandrovich laying the foundation of the Trans-Siberian Railway

Alexander III was very strict with the Romanov family. His children did not have any independence and he reduced the number of grand dukes. All relatives were the objects of the tsar's will and obliged to serve the nation. The emperor's word was law. One of his courtiers said that when the tsar spoke, "he gave the impression of being on the point of striking you."

Members of the Imperial family
at the Livadia palace. 1894

ganised by the Black Hundreds, the shooting of striking workers at the Lena Gold Mines (1912) and, finally, the First World War (1914). The tsar became known as "Nicholas the Bloody", although Russian blood continued to pour long after his abdication.

Like most people, Nicholas II was simply a mixture of good and bad. He has been variously described as "kind and extremely well brought-up" (Count Sergius Witte) and "a savage in love with the autocracy" (Vasily Klyuchevsky). The poet Alexander Blok perhaps best summed up his dilemma: "Stubborn

Funeral of Alexander III
in St Petersburg. 1894

Wedding of Tsar Nicholas II and Grand Duchess Alexandra Fedorovna. 1894.
Artist: Ilya Repin

yet weak-willed, nervy yet lackadaisical, harassed and cautious in speech, Nicholas II ceased to be his own master. Falling into the power of those whom he himself had appointed, he failed to understand the true nature of things or to take any decisive steps."

On 14 November 1894, Nicholas married Princess Victoria Alix Helena Louise Beatrice of Hesse-Darmstadt. The daughter of Grand Duke Louis IV of Hesse and Princess Alice of Great Britain, Nicholas's bride was the favourite granddaughter of Queen Victoria. She converted to Orthodoxy as Alexandra Fedorovna.

Alexander III had initially opposed the marriage, as Hesse had previously brought bad luck to Russia. Hessian princesses had been the wives of Paul I and Alexander II, who had both been murdered. The female line of Hesse carried an hereditary disease — haemophilia. Nicholas, however, insisted on marrying the woman he loved. Nicholas and Alexandra lived a life of quiet seclusion at Tsarskoe Selo. The tsar enjoyed spending time with his family, sawing and chopping

Imperial Regalia.
Artist: Nikolai Samokish

Nicholas and Alexandra were crowned in the Moscow Kremlin on 14 May 1896. The service was performed at the Dormition Cathedral by Metropolitan Palladius of St Petersburg, with the help of the metropolitans of Kiev and Moscow. Wearing their coronation robes, the tsar and tsarina led a procession to the Kremlin Palace. When they reached the top of the Red Stairway, they turned and bowed to the people.

Dish presented to Tsar Nicholas II by the Moscow District Zemstvo. 1896

Coronation Procession in Moscow.
14 May 1896

Nicholas II Crowning
Alexandra Fedorovna

wood, clearing away snow or going on long walks on foot. He also liked travelling by car, train or yacht and shooting crows in the park near the Imperial palace. The only thing he disliked was governing — unlike his wife, who constantly interfered in affairs of state, with disastrous consequences. Alexandra had been educated in England by her grandmother and studied philosophy at Heidelberg University. Dabbling in religious mysticism, she was an easy victim for various charlatans. The first was Mitka the Fool and his companion Elpidifor, who "interpreted" his mumblings. Mitka was followed by a demon-possessed woman called Daria Osipovna. Besides home-grown mystics, the empress also attracted a number of foreign occultists, including

Speech of His Imperial Highness to the Village Elders and Representatives of the Rural Population of Russia on 18 May 1896. After a watercolour by Ilya Repin

Alexandra Fedorovna with the Order of St Catherine. 1895. Artist: Ilya Galkin

Members of the House of Romanov in Tsarskoe Selo.
Mid-1890s

Anna Vyrubova.
1910s

Papus from Paris, Schenk from Vienna and Philippe from Lyon. Why did Alexandra Fedorovna turn to these people? The reason was her desire to give birth to a son. The dynasty needed a male heir and she had given birth to four daughters — Olga, Tatyana, Maria and Anastasia. Alexandra was so obsessed by the need to give birth to a boy that she allowed herself to be convinced that she was pregnant in 1903. She experienced all the symptoms of pregnancy and everyone awaited the birth of a son. When the time came, however, it proved to be the fruit of her imagination.

Russians remembered Alexander Pushkin's *Tale of Tsar Saltan*, the story of a queen who gives birth in the night to "not a son, not a daughter, not a mouse or frog, but an unknown little creature."

Nicholas II, Alexandra Fedorovna
and daughter Olga. 1896

Bedroom of Alexandra Fedorovna in the Alexander Palace
in Tsarskoe Selo

Alexandra Fedorovna
and son Alexei. 1904

Nicholas II
and son Alexei. 1904

In 1904, Alexandra Fedorovna finally gave birth to a son, whom his parents called Alexei. Their joy was short-lived, however, when they discovered that he had haemophilia.

Alexei's illness increased Alexandra's tendency to cut herself off from the rest of the world. Disgruntled courtiers muttered: "If she had her way, life would be one endless tea party at Tsarskoe Selo." In 1905, however, the tsarina made a new friend. This was Anna Taneyeva, a twenty-year-old lady-in-waiting.

Anna was a chubby girl with ash-coloured hair and enormous blue eyes. She was devoted to Alexandra, who liked her simple manners. The two women spent hours together, sharing

Grand Duchesses Tatyana and Maria in a Goat-Cart
in Tsarskoe Selo. 1902

secrets, singing duets or playing together on the piano. Alexandra called her "Anya", while Anna called her "Sana". Alexandra Fedorovna hoped that her young friend would be as happy in marriage as she was. She began looking for a husband and found one in the form of a naval officer called Alexander Vyrubov. Anna and Alexander were married in 1907. Unfortunately for Anna, Alexandra Fedorovna was a poor judge of people. Vyrubov turned out to be a drug addict and an impotent pervert. After several wretched months with her husband, Anna ran away from him, with the full support of Nicholas and Alexandra, who knew all the details of her unhappy marriage.

Alexei was a handsome little boy with blue eyes and golden curls, which later turned to auburn and became quite straight. His parents called him their "little ray of sun-

Daughters of Nicholas II
in St Petersburg. 1905

Tsarevich Alexei
in St Petersburg. 1907

shine." Before he was one year old, his father took him to a parade of the Preobrazhensky Guards. The soldiers greeted him with a resounding "hurrah" and the infant gurgled with delight. When he was one, his mother took him for a carriage ride and was delighted to see people along the road bowing and smiling to the young heir. Alexei grew up into

On one of the avenues in the park at Peterhof.
1896

Empress and her daughter Tatyana.
Photograph in Fabergé frame. 1898

Alexander Mosolov, director of the court chancellery, on Bloody Sunday: "The events of 9 January 1905 are too well known to be repeated here. That day, I was astonished at the senseless and aimless attacks of the cavalry on the crowd and the inequity of the commands issued by the chiefs." According to the official figures, ninety-six people were killed and 330 were injured. The unofficial reports suggest that 4,900 people suffered. The families of the dead were given one thousand roubles in compensation.

Father Gapon at the opening of the Kolomna branch of the trade union of factory workers. November 1904

Workers Shot by Tsarist Forces on Palace Square on 9 January 1905

an intelligent, observant, kind and lively individual. He did not enjoy studying and obeyed only his father. Upon learning that he was the heir to the throne, he said: "When I am tsar, there will be no poor or unhappy people. I want everyone to be happy." During the First World War, Nicholas took him to army headquarters, where he slept alongside his father on a camp bed.

On 14 May 1905, the Russian fleet encountered the Japanese navy in the Strait of Tsushima between Japan and Korea. The Russian squadron was commanded by Admiral Rozhestvensky and consisted of 30 warships with 228 guns. The Japanese fleet was commanded by Admiral Togo and had 121 warships with 910 guns. Besides numerical superiority, the Japanese navy also had more powerful guns, thicker armour and faster ships. The loss of the Russian fleet at the Battle of Tsushima meant defeat in the Russo-Japanese War. In August 1905, Russia and Japan signed a peace treaty at Portsmouth in the United States. Under the peace terms, Japan was awarded South Sakhalin, several islands and the lease on Port Arthur

Battle of Tsushima. 1905.
Artist: A. Tron

On 17 October 1905, Nicholas II signed a manifesto promising to create a parliament or Duma. The Duma met at the Tauride Palace in St Petersburg between 1906 and 1917. There was a total of four sessions. The First Duma lasted 72 days, while the Second Duma lasted 101 days. Both were dissolved by the tsar and many deputies were arrested.

Sitting of the Fourth Duma
at the Tauride Palace. Between 1912 and 1914

Peter Stolypin.
St Petersburg. 1907

and surrounding waters. When the Soviet Union established diplomatic relations with Japan in 1925, the Communists recognised the Treaty of Portsmouth, while refusing to bear political responsibility for the agreement. After the Japanese capitulation in the Second World War, South Sakhalin and the Kuril Islands were returned to Russia. The Church of the Resurrection of Christ was built in 1907

Religious procession celebrating the consecration of the Church of the Resurrection of Christ in St Petersburg. 1907

Alexandra Fedorovna laying the foundations of the School of Folk Art in St Petersburg. 1914

Tsarevich Alexei
in Finland. 1912

Launch of the *Victory* at the Baltic Shipyard
in St Petersburg. 1900

on the bank of the Catherine Canal in St Petersburg, where Tsar Alexander II had been fatally wounded in 1881. The building was popularly known as the Church of the Saviour on Spilt Blood. The church was designed by architect Alfred Parland and archimandrite Ignatius in the neo-Russian style, recreating the Muscovite architecture of the sixteenth and seventeenth centuries. Construction work was overseen by Grand Duke Vladimir Alexandrovich, uncle of the tsar and president of the

Aurora cruiser
in 1904

Imperial Academy of Arts. The church had nine cupolas and could hold 1,600 people. It took twenty-three years and ten months to build, costing a grand total of 4,718,786 roubles and 31½ kopecks, which exceeded the original budget by over a million roubles. The official committee of investigation laid the blame on the conference secretary

In 1913, there were 2,585 automobiles on the roads of St Petersburg — 221 were government property, 328 were taxis and the rest belonged to private individuals or firms. The first highway code was published in 1901, establishing a speed limit of twelve versts or eight miles an hour.

Nicholas II Accepting a Parade on Board the *Prince Suvorov* at the Baltic Shipyard in St Petersburg. 1902

of the Imperial Academy of Arts, who was put on trial and sent to prison. After the loss of the Russian fleet in the Far East, a nationwide collection was held to reequip the Baltic Fleet with new ships, as only old vessels remained after the main squadron had sailed to the Pacific Ocean. By 1914, the Baltic Fleet had five battleships, ten cruisers, fifty-nine destroyers, twenty-three torpedo boats and its own air force.

In the last ten years before the First World War, the Russian budget enjoyed a surplus of 2,400,000,000 roubles — despite the lowering of the cost of railway travel and the abolition of the system of redemption payments.

A costume ball was held at the Winter Palace on 13 February 1903. Nicholas, Alexandra and the other guests were dressed in robes from the reign of Tsar Alexis (1645–76). The ball began with a concert in the Hermitage Theatre, followed by dancing in the Pavilion Room. The dances were

Study of Nicholas II in the Alexander Palace at Tsarskoe Selo

Nicholas II and Alexei in St Petersburg. 1913

Members of the Imperial family wearing clothes from the reign
of Tsar Alexis at the last Imperial costume ball on 13 Febuary 1903

Crest and emblem of the Empress
Alexandra Fedorovna

choreographed by Josef Kschessinski,
a soloist of the Imperial Ballet. The
ladies formed reels, while the gentlemen performed a *danse russe*. There
were a total of 390 guests, including
sixty guardsmen. This was the last
Imperial ball in Russian history.

The celebrations marking the tercentenary of the Romanov dynasty began on the morning of 21 February
1913 with an artillery salute of thirty-
one rounds from the Peter and Paul
Fortress. The Patriarch of Antioch performed a special mass at the Kazan
Cathedral. Nevsky Prospekt was lined
with troops and crowds of people ea-
ger to catch a glimpse of the Imperial family. At midday, the Romanovs
emerged from Palace Square in open
carriages. Nicholas and Alexei were in
the first carriage, drawn by a pair of

A costume ball was held at the Winter Palace on 13 February 1903. Nicholas, Alexandra and the other guests were dressed in robes from the reign of Tsar Alexis (1645–76). The ball began with a concert in the Hermitage Theatre, followed by dancing in the Pavilion Room. The dances were choreographed by Josef Kschessinski, a soloist of the Imperial Ballet. The ladies formed reels, while the gentlemen performed a *danse russe*. There were a total of 390 guests, including sixty guardsmen. This was the last Imperial ball in Russian history.

Banquet menu during the celebrations of the tercentenary of the Romanov. 1913

Nicholas II and his children in the Kremlin during the tercentenary of the House of Romanov. 1913

horses. The second conveyed the two empresses — Alexandra Fedorovna and Maria Fedorovna — followed by the tsar's four daughters in a third carriage. The tsarevich was carried by a Cossack, his face contorted with pain. Alexandra Fedorovna had a cold and distracted air. The next day, a gala performance of Mikhail Glinka's opera *A Life for the Tsar* was given at the Mariinsky Theatre in the presence of the Imperial family, followed by a ball at the Noblemen's Assembly on 23 February.

1914

On 1 August 1914, Russia entered the First World War on the side of Britain and France against Germany and Austria-Hungary. The first action on the Eastern Front was the Russian attack on East Prussia and Galicia. The Germans were forced to remove several regiments from France and rush them to the east. Although her two armies in East Prussia were defeated, Russia enjoyed more success against Austria-Hungary. In spring 1915, Germany decided to concentrate on the Eastern Front. While the Russians lost Poland and parts of the Baltic territories, White Russia and the Ukraine, the Germans did not succeed in their main aim — to knock Russia out of the war. In 1916, Germany launched its main blow against France. Russia came to the assistance of the French by launching an offensive on the Eastern Front. General Alexei Brusilov broke through the Austro-Hungarian lines and Germany was again forced to remove troops from the Western Front to save her ally. In 1917, the Russian army was too demoralised to score any success in Galicia or White Russia. After the Bolsheviks seized power, they signed a peace treaty with the Central Powers in March 1918.

Nicholas and Alexandra found another new friend in 1905 — Grigory Rasputin. A peasant from the village of Pokrovskoe in Tobolsk Province, Rasputin is the hero of many works of fiction and non-fiction. In books and films, he is variously por-

Alexandra Fedorovna with her daughters Tatyana and Olga at Tsarskoe Selo. 1914

Nicholas II blessing soldiers leaving for the front

Christ Has Risen!
Easter Postcard. 1915

Nicholas II and Grand Duke Nikolai
Nikolaevich on manoeuvres. 1913

trayed as a lecherous drunkard or a mad
monk. The only thing that can be said
with any certainty now is that he was
able to ease the sufferings of the heir.
Outside the palace, Rasputin's drunk-
en excesses and scandalous love affairs
made him an inconvenient friend for the
Imperial family. From aristocrats and ministers
down to peasants and workers, the whole country dis-
cussed the possible relationships between Nicholas, Anna,
Rasputin and Alexandra. The "holy man" was said to have turned
the entire court into his private harem.

Felix and Irina Yussupov.
1910s

Yussupov Palace. 1830–38.
Architect: Andrei Mikhailov II

After Nicholas was overthrown in February 1917, the Provisional Government formed a special commission to investigate the "criminal actions" of the tsarist regime. They were particularly interested in the role and influence of Rasputin. Although the commission never completed its work, much of the evidence was later published. Vladimir Rudnev wrote about Anna Vyrubova: "The medical examination of Anna Vyrubova carried out in May 1917 by the extraordinary commission of investigation establishes beyond doubt that Anna Vyrubova was a virgin."

Rudnev wrote about Rasputin: "One of the most valuable sources throwing light on Rasputin's personality is the journal of the police agents who kept him under secret surveillance ... Rasputin's love affairs were confined to nocturnal orgies with girls of immoral character, cabaret singers and several of his female petitioners ... No evidence was found to confirm his proximity to members of the upper class." The problem was not just the presence of Anna or Rasputin in the royal

Grigory Rasputin with
his children. 1910s

Grigory Rasputin.
St Petersburg. 1909

Grigory Rasputin
with a group of admirers. 1910s

chambers — which had seen many colourful people throughout the three-hundred-year history of the Romanov dynasty. What angered the tsar's relatives and other members of the court was the way in which Rasputin interfered in the running of the government, particularly the appointment and dismissal of ministers. He was not simply disliked; he was loathed. Grand Duke Nikolai Nikolaevich, commander-in-chief of the Russian army, promised to hang him if he visited headquarters during the First World War. And it was Nikolai's wife, Anastasia, who had first introduced Nicholas and Alexandra to Rasputin. Rasputin's enemies, including two close relatives of the tsar — Grand Duke Dmitry Pavlovich and Prince Felix

The assassins before the murder of Grigory Rasputin.
Reconstruction

Yussupov — decided to kill the hated "holy man". On the night of 16/17 December 1916, he was lured to the Yussupov Palace on the River Moika and murdered in the basement. While Rasputin's demise evoked popular rejoicing throughout the country, this joy was short-lived. His death was merely the first in a long line of mass murders.

After the revolution, Anna Vyrubova was arrested and imprisoned in the Peter and Paul Fortress. In December 1920, she managed to escape to Finland, where she published her memoirs in response to a false "diary" written by Alexei Tolstoy and Pavel Schegolev. She died in Helsinki on 23 July 1964.

Prince Felix Yussupov and Grigory Rasputin before the murder.
Reconstruction

Body of Grigory Rasputin
on 17 December 1916

1917

In 1913, Russia celebrated the tercentenary of the Romanov dynasty. By then, however, it was clear that the autocracy was no longer relevant. Russia required other forms of government in response to the rapid industrialisation of the country in the late nineteenth and early twentieth centuries.

The Russian Empire suffered a series of heavy defeats during the First World War. The army began to disintegrate and the whole country was plunged into crisis. On International Women's Day, 23 February/8 March 1917, workers took to the

Grand Duke
Mikhail Alexandrovich. 1910

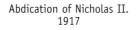

Abdication of Nicholas II.
1917

News of the overthrow of the autocracy reaches the front.
Spring 1917

Act of abdication of Grand Duke
Mikhail Alexandrovich. 3 March 1917

First cabinet of the Provisional Government.
March 1917

Alexander Kerensky
in the Winter Palace library. 1917

streets of Petrograd, demanding bread and an end to the war and the autocracy. On 27 February, the troops mutinied and went over to the workers, signalling the start of the revolution. The tsarist ministers were arrested and new organs of power were established. On 28 February, Nicholas II left army headquarters for Tsarskoe Selo, but his train was stopped by revolutionary troops.

On 2 March 1917, under the pressure of public opinion, Emperor Nicholas II abdicated in favour of his brother Mikhail and signed a manifesto of abdication.

Burning Tsarist emblems on Nevsky Prospekt.
February 1917

Nicholas II under arrest
at Tsarskoe Selo. 1917

The following day, Mikhail refused the throne, bringing the Romanov dynasty to an end. After Nicholas II abdicated, power passed into the hands of the Provisional Government. As he was both an admiral of the British navy (28 May 1908) and a field-marshal of the British army (16 February 1916), Russia suggested that Britain offer political asylum to the former tsar. When Nicholas's cousin, King George V of England, turned down this request, the Provisional Government decided it would be safer to remove the ex-tsar and his family to Tobolsk in Siberia.

Their position deteriorated after the Bolsheviks seized power in October 1917. Nicholas, Alexandra and their children were sent to Ekaterinburg, where they and their servants were shot in the basement of the Ipatiev House on the night of 16/17 July 1918. In 1991, human remains were discovered in a forest near Ekaterinburg. A Russian government commission ruled that they belonged to the former tsar, his family and servants. On 17 July 1998, the remains of Nicholas and Alexandra, their daughters Olga, Tatyana and Maria, Yevgeny Botkin (doctor), Anna Demidova (maid), Aloisy Trupp (valet) and Ivan Kharitonov (cook) were buried in the St Catherine Chapel of the St Peter and St Paul Cathedral. The funeral service was attended by President Boris Yeltsin and read by Father Boris Glebov, senior priest of the Peter and Paul Fortress. The names of Nicholas and his family were not mentioned in the prayers for the souls of the dead, as the church disagreed with the findings of the government commission.

On 14 August 2000, Nicholas II, Alexandra Fedorovna and all their children were canonised by the Russian Orthodox Church.

По распоряжению Областого
Исполнительного Комитета Советов
Рабочих, Крестьянских и Солдатских
Депутатов Урала и Рев, Штаба бывший

Царь и Самодержавец

Николай Романов

расстрелян

17 июля 1918 года.

г. Екатеринбург. 2

Весьма секретно

РАБОЧЕ-КРЕСТЬЯНСКОЕ
ПРАВИТЕЛЬСТВО
РОССИЙСКОЙ ФЕДЕРАТИВНОЙ РЕСПУБЛИКИ
СОВЕТОВ
УРАЛЬСКИЙ ОБЛАСТНОЙ СОВЕТ
РАБОЧИХ
КРЕСТЬЯНСКИХ И СОЛДАТСКИХ
ДЕПУТАТОВ
ПРЕЗИДИУМ

Протокол

Постановление о расстреле Царской Семьи от 14 июля 1918 г.

Ipatiev House in Ekaterinburg.
1970s

Nicholas II and family.
1913

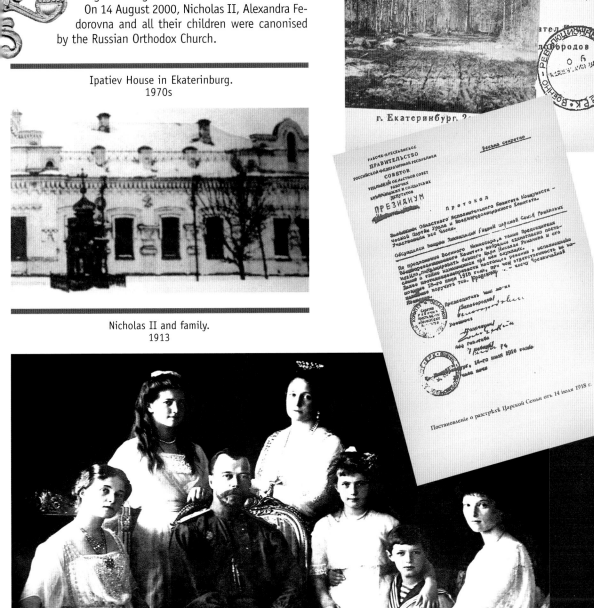

St Peter and St Paul Cathedral.
St Catherine's side chapel. Tombstone
on the graves of Emperor Nicholas II,
Empress Alexandra Fedorovna,
their children, the family's doctor
and their servants

The Establishment of Statehood. The Rurikid Princes   7

The First Russian Dynasty. The Rurikid Princes   21

     Grand Prince Ivan III Vasilyevich of Moscow and All Rus   22

     Grand Prince Basil III Ivanovich of Moscow and All Rus   26

     Grand Prince Tsar Ivan IV Vasilyevich the Terrible

     of Moscow and All Rus   28

     Tsar Fedor I   36

The Time of Troubles. Interregnum   43

     Tsar Boris Godunov   44

     Tsar Fedor Godunov   50

     Tsar False Dmitry I   52

     Tsar Basil IV Ivanovich Shuisky   54

The Second Russian Dynasty. The Romanovs   59

     Tsar Michael Fedorovich   60

     Tsar Alexei Mikhailovich   64

     Tsar Fedor II   72

     Regent Sophie   74

     Tsar Ioann V   76

     Emperor Peter I   78

     Empress Catherine I   92

     Emperor Peter II   96

     Empress Anna Ioannovna   98

     Regent Anna Leopoldovna. Emperor Ioann VI   102

     Empress Elizabeth Petrovna   104

     Emperor Peter III   110

     Empress Catherine II   112

     Emperor Paul I   118

     Emperor Alexander I   124

     Emperor Nicholas I   130

     Emperor Alexander II   136

     Emperor Alexander III   142

     Emperor Nicholas II   148

RUSSIAN TSARS

P-2 Art Publishers, St Petersburg

E-mail: info@p-2.ru